NURSES BRED FOR BUSINESS

THE AWAKENING OF LEGIONS OF NURSE ENTREPRENEURS

Robert C. Saunders RN

Published by Dynamically Activated, LLC

WHAT PEOPLE ARE SAYING

~ ~ ~ ~

In this book, Saunders successfully applies the concepts of business and takes it to the patient bedside. Historically, the training of the professional nurse is focused within the science of humanities, but after reading this analogy, perhaps a few more business courses should be included as part of the preparation of the RN. The author does an excellent job of highlighting the business skills from the world view of the nurse. This should encourage the blossoming nurse entrepreneur to move forward with his/her ideas and dreams.

Rhonda Anderson, MSN, RN, CCRN
Nursing Instructor

~ ~ ~ ~

I love Robert's confident ability to relate business to a nurse's life. Every nurse should absolutely make their innate skills work for them.

Stephanie Sharp, BSN, RN
Nurse Manager

This book describes events and strategies in business that worked for the author. Your results, business conditions and skill sets may be different. Before beginning a new career or starting a business, be sure to consult licensed professionals who are familiar with your particular situation and can provide you with advice that is specific to you.

NURSES BRED FOR BUSINESS

Cover designed by Telemachus Press, LLC

Cover art:
Copyright © iStock-507878462_shironosov
Copyright © iStock-629431156_Pablo_K

REALTOR® is a trademark of National Association of REALTORS®

Published by Dynamically Activated, LLC
204 37th Avenue N
Suite 310
St. Pete, FL 33704

Digital design by Telemachus Press, LLC
http://www.telemachuspress.com

Visit the author's websites:
http://www.dynamicallyactivated.com
http://www.nursesbred.com

Social Media Contacts:
https://www.facebook.com/Dynamically-Activated-264748394020044/
https://www.pinterest.com/dynamicallyactivated/pins/
https://www.linkedin.com/in/dynamically-activated-095342149/
https://www.instagram.com/dynamicallyactivated/

ISBN: 978-0-9982692-0-7 (eBook)
ISBN: 978-0-9982692-1-4 (Paperback)
ISBN: 978-0-9982692-2-1 (Hardcover)

Version 2017.09.21

DEDICATION

This book is dedicated to the many strong and proud nursing pioneers who paved the way for us and inspired this book such as Carol Elliot, Catherine Crumb, Wilhelmina Babcock, and Laura Gasparis Vonfrolio.

ACKNOWLEDGEMENTS

Special thanks go to Darlene Carroll and Sarita Banks for technical support, editing and proofreading. Cannot forget Sherry Blake for all of her undying support and the fanfare she has generated in my efforts thus far. I must also mention the many philanthropic kindnesses of the St Anthony's Hospital Foundation towards me and the important mission they serve in the local community and around the world. I absolutely must acknowledge my wife Victoria Saunders who gets more excited about my various projects than I do and as such she represents my heart.

TABLE OF CONTENTS

Part 3: 12 <u>MORE</u> Sure Fire Ways to Fail Miserably in Your 1st Year as a Real Estate Agent   73

NURSES BRED FOR BUSINESS

THE AWAKENING OF LEGIONS OF NURSE ENTREPRENEURS

PREFACE

After 21years of bedside nursing I began to notice a few trends Many nurses who felt like there was a need to do and be more went back to school for advanced degree(s). Curiously enough, many that I have conversed with took a dual masters path. They obtained both an Advance Nurse Practitioners Degree AND a Master's in Business Administration.

Others transitioned to other areas such as ER, critical care, administration or some other form of bedside nursing. Still others go the route of case management, nursing education and even home health or hospice care.

I also noticed those nurses who, for one reason or another had their licenses revoked!! WHAT NOW? How do these individuals survive and take care of families when their main source of income is pulled from under them?

Also, everyone in healthcare must open their eyes to the very real possibility of hospital closures. Don't believe it? I would never jokingly make such an assertion. In a 2014 USA

Today article entitled "Rural hospitals in critical condition" note the following:

Since the beginning of 2010, 43 rural hospitals—with a total of more than 1,500 beds—have closed, according to data from the North Carolina Rural Health Research Program. The pace of closures has quickened; from 3 in 2010 to 13 in 2013, and 12 already this year. Georgia alone has lost five rural hospitals since 2012, and at least six more are teetering on the brink of collapse. Each of the state's closed hospitals served about 10,000 people—a lot for remaining area hospitals to absorb.

The Affordable Care Act was designed to improve access to health care for all Americans and will give them another chance at getting health insurance during open enrollment starting this Saturday. But critics say the ACA is also accelerating the demise of rural outposts that cater too many of society's most vulnerable. These hospitals treat some of the sickest and poorest patients—those least aware of how to stay healthy. Hospital officials contend that the law's penalties for having to re-admit patients soon after they're released are impossible to avoid and create a crushing burden. "The stand-alone, community hospital is going the way of the dinosaur," says Angela Mattie, chairwoman of the health care management and organizational leadership department at Connecticut's Quinnipiac University, known for its public opinion surveys on issues including public health.

The closings threaten to decimate a network of rural hospitals the federal government first established beginning in the late 1940s to ensure that no one would be without health care. It was a theme that resonated during the push for the new health law. But rural hospital officials and others say that federal regulators—along with state governments—are now starving the hospitals they created with policies and reimbursement rates that make it nearly impossible for them to stay afloat.

Low Medicare and Medicaid reimbursements hurt these hospitals more than others because it's how most of their patients are insured, if they are at all. Here in Stewart County, it's a problem that expanding Medicaid to all of the poorest patients—which the ACA intended but 23 states including Georgia have not done, according to the federal government—would help, but wouldn't solve."

Between local hospitals closing, damaging congressional legislation, and our most at risk populations suddenly left without access to healthcare, one thing becomes evident; the realities of a seismic economic devastation crystallize before us.

Now, I don't bring these things to draw a dark cloud over healthcare or nursing in general. Instead I use these cold facts as a springboard for ushering in what could become the greatest vision of nursing's future: THE ERA OF THE NURSE ENTREPRENEUR

What do I mean by this?

According to the Bureau of Labor Statistics, U.S. Department of Labor, Occupational Outlook Handbook, 2016-17 Edition, registered nurses held about 2.8 million jobs in 2014. The industries that employed the most registered nurses were as follows:

Hospitals; state, local, and private—61% of registered nurses

Nursing and residential care facilities—7%
Offices of physicians—7%
Home healthcare services—6%
Government—6%

Registered nurses are the largest healthcare occupation. They work in hospitals, physicians' offices, home healthcare services, and nursing care facilities. Others work in schools or outpatient clinics, or serve in the military. Home health and public health nurses travel to patients' homes, schools, community centers, and other sites.

Some nurses move frequently, traveling in the United States and throughout the world to help care for patients in places where there are not enough healthcare workers.

What I am suggesting is that ALL nurses and by extension everyone working in healthcare take responsibility for the direction of their own financial vehicle.

How exciting would things become if an increasing number of nurses over time decided it was time to strike out and start their own business while still working initially. One could then parlay accumulated nursing knowledge and experience into monetary compensation of another sort!

What would this measure of newfound economic independence do for nurses?

- Create a future not completely dependent on whether the hospital closes or not.
- High potential of offering healthcare services and opportunities which face increasing demand whether hospitals, healthcare insurance or government funding exists or not.

- Position ourselves for capitalizing on billions of dollars to be had creating solutions to the toughest societal health challenges of tomorrow.

It is my desire that what you will encounter in the following chapters is a thought model attempting to transition:

Core nursing activities = to equivocal = Core business activities

This will showcase that healthcare knowledge workers are really bred or prepped for business in an unscripted future.

PART 1

GETTING DOWN TO BUSINESS

CHAPTER 1
THE NURSE OWNER, CEO AND ENTREPRENEUR

OWNER

Right from the outset of this chapter title it has always been the expectation of administration and patients that the nurse own EVERYTHING! This being the case whether what happens is your fault or not. Fortunately, our training and temperament makes us well suited to successfully tackle prob lems, make effective decisions and take a team approach to solution attainment. Each of the many failures we encounter over time are the training wheels for greater future successes.

I will also add that any failures you don't learn from or are not transformed by will only hamstring any potential fu ture success and opportunities that may come across your table. Please continue to grow from each failure. In speaking with many long-lived nurse, the only difference between the nurse still practicing and those no longer in nursing is that the experienced nurse lived to tell the tale. As a result, their in credible experiences went on to define them.

CEO

One definition of a Chief Executive Officer and responsibilities:

> "Top executive responsible for a firm's overall operations and performance. He or she is the leader of the firm, serves as the main link between the board of directors (the board) and the firm's various parts or levels, and is held solely responsible for the firm's success or failure. One of the major duties of a CEO is to maintain and implement corporate policy as established by the board. Also called President or managing director, he or she may also be the chairman (or chairperson) of the board."

Many of the expectations of nursing are directly translatable to starting and running your own business. Just think thru the course of your atypical day where one deals only in constantly changing circumstances wears multiple hats. As a nurse, you are responsible for intelligently guiding patient education, preserving patient dignity, championing patient advocacy, maximizing the quality and value of patient care delivery. All the while being constantly looked upon to lead or guide others toward achieving a common mission. In this striving and doing and being emerges the nurse's constitutive nature and substance as the servant leader.

Leadership is an expansive term that is as old as man himself and is still the subject of great research and debate. Essentially, everyone is in a role of being a leader, whether you're responsible for yourself and one patient in achieving certain daily outcomes related to your organizations mission, vision and values or for all the staff and patients on hospital property.

Attaining to victory in one area can carry over to victory in all areas. So as a servant leader, what will be your personal corporation's mission and vision? Will it be compelling enough to pull you out of bed to clock in early and keep you up at night? What valuable product or service will you bring to the marketplace? By serving the greater good of others one serves his or herself, the basis of all great entrepreneurial endeavors.

Since you are also a Chief Executive Officer of your own life, you will be responsible to your board of directors and charged with maximizing the value of your corporation or Limited Liability Company (LLC). If you are on your own board of directors and are fully responsible for your enterprises' success, would you hire or fire yourself right now? Other responsibilities of a CEO involve decision making actions that lead to execution and management of strategy when it comes to daily operations.

Regardless of level of nursing or business education, skill sets, etc. at the outset of your startup you will wear all the hats and need to think expansively as nurses do. This will include all sectors and fields of the business: operations, marketing, business development, finance, human resources, etc. If this sounds like a tall order, that's because it is.

ENTREPRENEUR
This term of entrepreneur I had woven together in my mind with the term CEO as being one in the same until I came across the fascinating origin of the word.

Entrepreneur (n.)

1828, "manager or promoter of a theatrical production," reborrowing of French entre-preneur "one who undertakes or manages," agent noun from Old French entreprendre "undertake"

Source: OnLine Entymology Dictionary, ©2001-2017 Douglas Harper; reprinted with permission.

According to sources this word was coined by French economist Jean-Baptiste Say. What do these entrepreneurs do? They use their "industry" (a term Say prefers to "labor") to organize and direct the factors of production so as to achieve the "satisfaction of human wants." But they are not merely managers. They are forecasters, project appraisers, and risk takers as well. Out of their own financial capital, or that borrowed from someone else, they advance funds to the owners of labor, natural resources ("land") and machinery ("tools"). These payments or "rents" are recouped only if the entrepreneurs succeed in selling the product to consumers. Entrepreneurial success is not only sought after by the individual, but also essential to the society as a whole. A country well stocked with intelligent merchants, manufacturers, and agriculturists has more powerful means of attaining prosperity, than one devoted chiefly to the pursuit of the arts and sciences."

Essentially, entrepreneurs seek out inefficient uses of resources and capital and move them into more productive, higher yield areas.

Say thus painted the picture of an economic adventurer as an agent of change. I love this new expanded definition as it resonated well with a rapidly changing global economy that has propelled us into the Age of the Entrepreneur. Each individual will ultimately experience their own industrial revolution, ready or not.

Fortunately, nursing as an industry has been grooming us all along. Now we must apply the same success methodologies and powerful work ethic that we attained as a high achiever working for an employer and apply it systematically to expanding your own economy.

As we progress onward we will see more of this nursing to business convergence that will inspire hope and confidence.

For example, think through your daily business activity as you would a typical day working in a hospital setting.

- Punch In: Arrive early to mentally prepare yourself and demonstrate that you're emotionally invested in the outcome.

- Round Up with staff: Relatively new to many hospital settings, this ritual powwow with staff and management that sets the tone for the day's agenda and latest focus on what is priority and what is not.

- Each patient: each patient is a Business Unit. The hospital having had a much bigger head start has invested millions and perhaps even billions in infrastructure to ensure that they can orchestrate the management of hundreds of beds (one business unit per bed).

Join me in Chapter 2 as we expand on this thought of business management.

CHAPTER 2
EACH PATIENT IS A BUSINESS UNIT

Regardless of how people romanticize the nurturing spiritual aspects of patient centered care, it is at its core a for profit enterprise driven by fast moving macro and microeconomic forces that no one in business can choose to conveniently ignore.

That being said we will now explore the many similarities that each patient represents from a purely business point of view.

To start with each Hospital is a microcosm or a miniaturized version of the local or national economy. If people perceive that the economy is bad or that their personal financial circumstances are bad they are not going to come to the hospital or call 911, even if they are very sick. Less patients means less consumers of healthcare products and services which comes to less demand for nursing and support staff. This is bad for business.

The Emergency Medical Service (EMS) is a beautiful lead generator with foot traffic that directs a constant funnel of increasing contacts—paying customers with stress on paying—to the emergency center. No matter what, rain or shine, the equivalent of ambulances representing continual overriding customer demand must always be lining up at your business door! If you're buying a business from someone and there is not a database of paying satisfied customers, then you don't have a business! In addition, there must be lead generation systems in place to continue to expand your business so that YOU are the 911 call center of your market sector 24/7.

Right here is the crux of ALL business!! If a business does not have a customer acquisition system and budget for efficiently and effectively acquiring a widening database of customers, then you don't have a business that a business broker could package and sell profitably. If there are no customers/patients there is no cash flow. No cash flow, no revenue. No revenue, no profits. No profits, then hospitals close their doors permanently in most cases.

THE BUSINESS UNIT REVISITED

Nowhere else does the capacity of the hospital to scale or increase its size, performance or number of users more than in the emergency center. The emergency center is where the cost of customer acquisition comes into play by stabilizing the newly acquired lead and acclimating them to our systems and processes in a value-added manner. This puts them at ease and makes them want to stay even though they would rather be elsewhere.

When the customer is admitted, now is the time to upsell to better service and products, constantly negotiating and upgrading to higher price points with the ultimate goal of undying customer loyalty. Dominating in this category requires we achieve world class marketing campaigns that deliver remarkable experiences and phenomenal results.

Now that the business unit has arrived to your floor, a small army of staff all armed with rolling computers that all have a robust CRM (customer relationship management) platform for charting arrive at the patient bedside.

Since the business unit has been down for any number of diagnosable reasons, the team's goal is to get the business back on its feet and back in action as soon as possible. Every moment that it is not running translates to mounting overhead expenses and rapidly shrinking return on investment. It is for this reason that the HMO/PPO's hold healthcare organizations to metrics such as diagnostic related groups (DRG's) and length of stay parameters with aggressive follow up by armies of case managers and social workers. In an era of rapidly shrinking reimbursement cost containment is king!!

The CRM and other systems in place allow for everyone to remain intimately connected with all of the business unit's vital statistics. Routine multisystem checks are the equivalent of the profit and loss statement. This data-driven term is so important to the life of any business anywhere on the planet that it deserves a formally defined introduction. Investopedia.com gives the following:

Statement of revenue and expenditures: A document showing the amount of profit earned minus the amount of operating expenses. The difference is reported as a profit or loss usually quarterly or annually.

Balance sheet: A condensed statement that shows the financial position of an entity on a specified date (usually the last day of an accounting period). Among other items of information, a balance sheet states (1) what assets the entity owns, (2) how it paid for them, (3) what it owes (its liabilities), and (4) what is the amount left after satisfying the liabilities. Balance sheet data is based on a fundamental accounting equation (assets = liabilities + owners' equity), and is classified under subheadings such as current assets, fixed assets, current liabilities, Long-term Liabilities. With income statement and cash flow statement, it comprises the set of documents indispensable in running a business.

Intake and output = Income and expenses and in this scenario the business unit has permission to have as much income as it wants. Labs let us know what the status of assets the unit is holding onto verses nasty liabilities.

The end game is to constantly increase revenue and expand assets while simultaneously reducing overhead expenses and shrink liabilities. Having an accounting system in place, be it paper or preferably computer software, that is accessible online by a competent and business savvy account is mission critical.

Staff meetings are those hateful but necessary pauses where everyone on the team can connect and refocus on what is game changing and what is not. It also is a reality check of mounting and unreasonable demands that come with playing on the playground of an international marketplace. This opportunity should not to be missed to brainstorm new tactics and strategy tapping the brain capital of everyone invested in the success of the enterprise.

CHAPTER 3
THE SPECIALISTS

Increasingly in situations where one or more of a unit's business systems are out of place, systems analysts or specialists are called in for no other purpose than to get the business units mind right. Only a whole individual, a whole or completely synergized business unit can bring its God honest best to the business table as the business is the mere extension of the person. In other words, get the person right and you get the business right. As your business acumen or skill grows in these areas and/or you know whom to go to for answers and you don't make it a habit of consulting too late in the game when the unit is taking its last breath. In many ways you will be able to fill the role of any of these following specialists.

A psychologist: Or a business coach may be brought in to deal with the psychological damage of past business relationships. Violated trust, broken alliances, embezzlement of funds, undercapitalization in the face of mounting cost of doing business can get just about drive anyone to give up hope of problem resolution.

An Orthopedic Surgeon: Or business consultant may be consulted in the event of broken supply chains, weak or disjointed marketing plans, etc. Essentially anything that is not necessarily life threatening at the outset, yet, can represent extreme losses in productivity for every moment down along with lengthy rehabilitation to get business the unit fully back on its feet.

A cardiologist: May be consulted on a beat to beat basis if the entire business is not being properly flushed with regular infusions of capital. He or she may require more specialized lab work and more high-end professional grade diagnostic tools to identify and repair blockages that if not addressed could be a sudden game ending affair. Time is money as well as the capacity to generate money one beat of the businesses day to day operations at a time.

A neurologist: Or chief technology officer may be needed in the event of some major impairment or gross inadequacies in the communicative capacity of your business unit's nerve center. It is possible that while your fiscal nervous system should be moving at the speed of thought, instead it may be on the verge of a massive stroke or nervous breakdown. Again the diagnostic equivalent of an MRI may be needed emergently. Each moment of time that passes sacrifices potential profits as well as present and future speed at which financial transactions can occur on your website, computers, or any electronic device critical to your entrepreneurial health.

Occupational, physical or speech therapists: Or business therapist/entrepreneurial mentor necessary to assess propensity for viable business unit salvage. In so doing, systematically optimizing the business unit to its most functional and profitable potential.

Case manager and social worker: Or business brokers will barter for outpatient outsourcing options that are the equivalent of long-term care or Hospice IF it has been determined that the business unit has poor outcomes associated across the board.

Pastoral care: Or business coach/corporate therapist can help all parties invested through the grieving process. Part of you is dying with this business unit because you invested a piece of yourself in striving for a successful conclusion that was never realized. You must let go at some point and move on to other opportunities.

CHAPTER 4
THE SERIAL ENTREPRENEUR, INFORMATION TECHNOLOGY AND WEBSITE MITOSIS

THE SERIAL ENTREPRENEUR

The one thing that I keep noticing over time at work was that I was more efficient, focused and productive in the hospital work environment than I was at my home office. So eventually I stopped and pondered why?

What I noticed was what I call for lack of a better term synergy. Synergy according to Merriam-Webster.com is simply defined as the increased effectiveness that results when two or more people or businesses work together. Another way to put it is combined action or operation. This developed over time among all the team members utilizing the same set of skills, tools, equipment and technologies. As a result, this allowed us not just to take care of one business unit, but 16 to 32 business units at a time per floor!

More often than not, each nurse is responsible for 4 to 6 business units at a time and is expected to not miss a beat!! It is not a coincidence that the any economy in the world that a business operates in has the same demands and expectations.

It is from this birthing chamber and often baptism by fire that I assert unflinchingly that nurses are bred for success, groomed for entrepreneurial greatness by default. This was not what was asked for, yet it was still conferred upon us. The late great actor Carroll O'Connor in one of his last movie roles made a profound statement when giving his grand-daughter some sage advice. He said to her "God gives the greatest challenges to those with the strongest will" ... *I REST MY CASE*!!

Whether you want to look at each hospital business unit as a franchise or as completely separate business entities with different needs and capacities is immaterial. Maybe you have seen stories of the individual that started with one Domino's pizza 30 years ago and now own 45 Domino's franchises. That person took the time to learn his craft and stayed focus long enough and worked diligently enough to now see fantastic results. In all that I promote, work will never be engineered out of ANY moneymaking venture you may pursue. Doesn't matter if you work for an employer or work for yourself, you will and must work.

INFORMATION TECHNOLOGY
Information technology is by definition a set of tools, processes, and methodologies (such as coding/programming, data communications, data conversion, storage and retrieval, systems analysis and design, systems control) and associated equipment employed to collect, process, and present information. In broad

terms, IT also includes office automation, multimedia, and telecommunications.

With a proper professional grade business platform in place of trained employees, systems of measurement and accountability, and even modest technological infrastructure (laptop, fax machine, printer, smart phone and Square Up device that turns a smart phone into a cash register) a sole entrepreneur can become a serial entrepreneur in the same synergistic breath. So give yourself every technological advantage possible as a matter of course.

At this time, it only seems right to address the subject of having a website built and properly integrated into accelerating business growth and profitability.

To best describe the purpose of a website first, I want to briefly touch on basic cellular biology. All of you may recall cell mitosis. Mitosis is one of two ways that cells divide and reproduce which enables cellular growth and repair in multicellular organisms. More specific to this discussion: a cell at some point in its maturation phase makes an exact clone of itself!

A website is a virtual living breathing organism that comes into being for the sole purpose of attracting leads (virtual foot traffic driven by effective marketing campaigns at x cost per customer/cost per click). It too must undergo regular growth and repair by translating to budgets for webhosting, search engine optimization and upgrades to its capacity to create multiple profit centers in addition to affiliate marketing.

At some point in the cellular websites business maturation phase it must divide into a second website, either still

supporting the current business unit or becoming a spinoff of
an altogether different, standalone financial entity. When this
happens, it will not be unusual to have 6, 12, 24 websites
sprawling across the world wide web extending its fiscal reach
to new markets with new products and new alliances forged.

If I have not yet convinced you as to the benefits ac-
crued to you by forming a website yesterday then I don't
know what more to say. Lastly, all entrepreneurs in the 21st
century are social media savvy and social media heavy or develop relationships with those who are proficient at such
things.

CHAPTER 5
BUSINESS UNITS BEHAVING BADLY AND EMERGENCY CODES

It is not just your imagination that hospital systems have whole in-house departments dedicated to promoting safety, onsite security guards, IT firewalls to stop cyber assaults and risk management. These cold realities must be seriously and deeply pondered and addressed with legally well-crafted policies and procedures that will in the long run cover your posterior features... Also, let us not leave out a constantly evolving company intranet to rapidly communicate reminders, changes and emerging threats.

EMERGENCY CODES
With time, someone had enough insight to develop emergency response codes that once announced overhead addresses internal and external threats to a productive business environment that must be acted upon immediately. The following is by no means an exhaustive list of relevant business crises that warrant definitive proactive courses of action.

Code Red: Put out potential fires STAT!

What is the point of investing massive assets, time and energy in a profitable business only to see all your efforts go up in smoke? To be clear, I am not just talking about literal fires but 4 alarm matters, which if not addressed on an hour by hour, day by day basis will bring down your whole business. Business liability insurance, government employee compliance matters, quarterly IRS tax submissions, and operating in the proper legal structures are vital risk mitigation and risk avoidance strategies to be taken seriously. The alternative to not having these measures in place is a viable business that could virtually go down in flames tomorrow.

Code Blue: Nothing lives without a pulse!

Who is responsible for assessing both the business unit's systems and its continuous heart rhythm? Without sufficient infusions of capital into the business unit, is it possible that last minute extraordinary efforts to regain a life sustaining pulse and heart beat are too little too late? This is why the habit of routinely running daily profit and loss strips on your business units and measuring out moment to moment where the dollars and cents are going will prevent bleeding out of precious capital.

Code Pink: Protect your baby at ALL costs!

You may not necessarily deal with child abductions revolving around your business unit, but your business unit is your baby! So it is something that you want to protect from predatory lenders, cyber hijacking of mission critical proprietary data, well-guarded trade secrets, embezzlement of corporate funds, etc., etc. Having the equivalent of a robust campus wide lock down will be a strong deterrent against such perverted fiscal insurgents.

Code Green: Effective disaster strategies life-saving!
A business unit disaster plan must be multifocal in scope with clear delegation of what to do in the event of flood, tornado, evacuation procedures. Is their safe offsite or onsite storage for corporate documents that cannot be replaced? Protection of business equipment? Commercial business insurance to cover losses incurred? Key man insurance in concert with a business continuity plan that allows the business to operate in spite of your death or absence? This is, I must say, the proverbial Holy Grail of all business owners. A business system that can run without your physical presence is ultimately what will allow you to run multiple businesses and continue adding multiple income streams with time.

Code Silver: Vigilant response to safety threats externally!
These are the days of the active shooter. What physical measures will you take to protect your business units from very real emerging threats? Especially if you are running a bricks and mortar establishment with lots of foot traffic and lawyers adding insult to injury by suing vulnerable business that have little or no security measures in place to ensure the safety of its patrons.

Lastly, I just want to add on the subject of policy, does everyone who touches the business unit have a clearly defined role? No one that works on or in your business should guess at what is expected of them. Do those that you would employ have a job description that would allow you to replace that person's job function to be filed quickly in the event of firing, sickness, etc.? Can present and future customers recognize these roles by dress and grooming? Scripting? Name badges? Uniforms and or uniform colors?

Code Grey: Vigilant response to safety threats internally!
This could be a reality show unto itself; unruly, disrespectful, entitled business units creating needless drama and threats to physical safety, not to mention embarrassing themselves and those who love them. What happens now if your business unit halls off and cold cocks one of your support staff or worse yet physically or sexually assaults another business unit? You thought you already had problems? Wait until the news media and armies of opportunistic attorneys get wind of this. One frivolous lawsuit could destroy everything you have built to date. Again, good security measures will also mitigate public relations nightmares along with well-crafted legal representation. This is the equivalent of 4-point-leather restraints and heavy-sedation strategies to effectively and humanely restore order and balance of power.

CHAPTER 6

FOUNDATIONS AND RAISING BUSINESS CAPITAL

THE FOUNDATION

Thus far, it has been my observation that many of the most successful hospital systems ultimately start up or team up with a foundation under whose auspices can push forward the company's mission; make more money!

An excellent and expanding pool of affluent donors, fundraisers, favorable marketing and media attention to expand corporate brand awareness and foundation sponsored events ensure a steady stream of working capital that keeps hospital doors open and interests expanding to add capacity for more business units. This is symbiosis, forged business alliances mutually beneficial to each other at its finest.

The next best question to ask is: how does one find themselves in these equitable terms? I don't believe that this merger was at all by accident. I would surmise that these two powerful yet compelling forces were attracted to each other and found and an immediate and substantive need to synergize. Just as a

living cells natural embedded function is to propagate life, the
natural maturation process of business is to seek alliances to
promote greater profitability and sustained patterns of economic growth.

RAISING BUSINESS CAPITAL
If raising raw cash is the only string that you know how to
work with then there are entire books written on attracting
and procuring needed capital in both traditional and creative
financing forms. Hence, I would recommend local commercial lending institutions, your local library, Chamber of
Commerce or searching "Dr. Google" for a cure for your
fiscal malady. There is yet another way to think through the
perceived obstacle of raising capital.

I love watching nature programs that are rife with sym-
biotic relationships or mutually beneficial alliances. One of my
favorite is the rhino and the oxpecker. The rhino gives the
oxpecker bird protection from its natural predators and in turn
the oxpecker keeps the large inflexible rhinos free of burrowing
ticks. If we think hard enough and in terms broad enough we
can think of mutually beneficial ways to advance each other's
business unit agenda that doesn't involve just money. It can
involve joining your businesses industry association or guild by
bartering say equipment for services or exchanging IT use for
free rental office or storage space. I can only say remove limits
on your imagination and brainstorming ability.

One exercise I have come across and use almost daily is:
How can I accomplish moving key business actions and goals
forward without money? Now, let's also look at OTHER
creative aspects.

Aside from OTHER PEOPLE'S MONEY, in the context of raising business capital, there are:

OTHER PEOPLE'S TIME
OTHER PEOPLE'S RESOURCES
OTHER PEOPLE'S KNOWLEDGE
OTHER PEOPLE'S EXPERIENCES
OTHER PEOPLE'S SKILLSETS
OTHER PEOPLE'S IMAGINATIONS
OTHER PEOPLE'S STRENGTHS
OTHER PEOPLE'S MOTIVATIONS
OTHER PEOPLE'S CHARISMA
OTHER PEOPLE'S LOOKS
OTHER PEOPLE'S INVENTIONS
OTHER PEOPLE'S NETWORKS
OTHER PEOPLE'S DATABASES
OTHER PEOPLE'S SCRIPTS
OTHER PEOPLE'S WEBSITES
OTHER PEOPLE'S BOOKS
OTHER PEOPLE'S BLOGGINGS
OTHER PEOPLE'S MERCHANDISE
OTHER PEOPLE'S SUPERCONNECTIONS
OTHER PEOPLE'S PLATFORMS
OTHER PEOPLE'S REAL ESTATE
OTHER PEOPLE'S MARKETING
OTHER PEOPLE'S MARKET RESEARCH
OTHER PEOPLE'S SYSTEMS
OTHER PEOPLE'S COACHING
OTHER PEOPLE'S WEALTH…

You get the idea that business is also about tapping the creativity, innovation, imagination, etc., of yourself and others. In unity, what can't be accomplished? What is more, this new way of thinking through problems and challenges instead of being crippled by them is transformational. It is this thinking that in actuality meets the definition of the raw entrepreneurial spirit—that of taking something from an area of low yield to an area of high yield. Seeing optimistically what others perceive as permanent obstacles is what makes nurse leaders into business leaders of the future.

I cannot think of a better time to equivocate other concepts of ethical behavior and code of conduct. Just as with any industry or field of endeavor there are bad along with the good.

> Unethical nurse = ethical business person?
> Not likely.
> Ethical nurse = unethical business leader?
> Don't buy it.
> Ethical nurse = ethical business practices?
> Yes, the message and the messenger are one package deal.

Let's just be clear about the fact that accountability is built into anything we strive for in life. Being in business for yourself only escalates in degrees of accountability. You must hold yourself accountable and ultimately responsible for any success or failure. Then when your business operation expands as it matures you also will be accountable to future employees, other businesses, boards of directors, shareholders, customers, the government, and so on and so forth. Your example on the frontiers of nursing translated to business will become a steadying force for diligent work ethic, integrity, good stewardship, and philanthropy. It may be around this time that some foundation or Chamber of Commerce will be drawn to your propensity for attracting and capitalizing upon new opportunities.

Lastly, as a matter of nursing entrepreneurial convergence, the number of cash flow sources you create should mimic the number of business units on the floor that you now work on. Allow me to repeat that, if you have 30 patients on your floor you should strive for 30 streams of income!! This is the natural progression of wealth creation and will ensure that your economic future is NOT governed by climatic market gyrations and layoffs. If you cannot manage $100 dollars then you cannot manage $10 million. One cash flow stream should become two, then four and so on allowing you over time to eventually become your own source of capital funding.

CHAPTER 7
KNOWLEDGE WORKERS AND
EVIDENCE BASED BUSINESS

KNOWLEDGE WORKERS
Knowledge work is defined as a job, process, or task that is distinguished by its specific information content or requirement. A knowledge worker is by extension defined as employees such as data analysts, product developers, planners, programmers, and researchers who are engaged primarily in acquisition, analysis, and manipulation of information as opposed to in production of goods or services. Popularized by the US management guru Peter Drucker (born 1909, in Austria).

Why this dictionary source left out nurses who meet every single aspect of what constitutes working with every aspect of the knowledge working game is beyond me. All day long nurses analyze the validity of actionable data, develop plans of action, continually are called upon to create, implement and modify workable business unit models in terms of efficient workflow, cost containment, strategize satisfactory multitier business metrics, etc. Lately, ever more so, nurses are called upon to research all manner of evidence based analysis, are at the hub of clinical and pharmaceutical research trials. Nursing is becoming so education centric that continuing education and the push toward advanced degrees as a default of minimum educational requirements is approaching rapidly on the horizon. This scholastic evolution has led to the emergence of nursing informatics.

The following definition of nursing informatics was pulled from amia.org academic forum:

> Nursing Informatics is the *"science and practice (that) integrates nursing, its information and knowledge, with management of information and communication technologies to promote the health of people, families, and communities worldwide."* (IMIA Special Interest Group on Nursing Informatics 2009).

The application of nursing informatics knowledge is empowering for all healthcare practitioners in achieving patient centered care.

Nurse informaticians work as developers of communication and information technologies, educators, researchers, chief nursing officers, chief information officers, software engineers, implementation consultants, policy developers, and business owners, to advance healthcare. Core areas of work include:

- Concept representation and standards to support evidence-based practice, research, and education

- Data and communication standards to build an interoperable national data infrastructure
- Research methodologies to disseminate new knowledge into practice
- Information presentation and retrieval approaches to support safe patient centered care
- Information and communication technologies to address inter-professional work flow needs across all care venues
- Vision and management for the development, design, and implementation of communication and information technology
- Definition of healthcare policy to advance the public's health

This worm hole goes pretty deep as the principles of informatics can be applied to any field of endeavor that one decides to focus upon, including...

EVIDENCE BASED BUSINESS

The transition from medical knowledge discovery and data mining in order to make effective lifesaving nursing decisions to seamlessly traversing market research data and mining key elements critical to sustaining healthy business units has never been clearer.

Operating in today's business climate, by necessity, dictates tapping into multiple industry journals from general to niche-specific. Everyone must have a finger on the pulse of your business, your industry and the world economy since the internet, social media and telecommunications has shrunk the world to a small neighborhood.

To simply stay relevant, it did not surprise me when business leaders such Warren Buffet and his lifelong business partner Charles Munger regularly took knowledge vacations!! These were for the sole purpose of soaking up as much information on issues facing their businesses as possible, then formulating multiple strategies and what if scenarios for effectively maneuvering around obstacles to sustained profitability. This pause likewise reveals numerous opportunities that others simply would not realize if they are simply going thru the motions of caring for business units without brains.

Good thing nurses are not afraid of great challenges or work. Your work is definitely cut out for you in the form of regular data dumps of market statistics, theoretical models, new and radically different ways of approaching and doing what you do. The same need to constantly ask the right questions and seek the best answers for the successful management of your business units also applies.

With regard to evidence-based business in your niche market (in which you should rightly seek to establish dominance), ask yourself:

- What are your competitors doing?
- Non-competitors?
- Who is failing?
- Why are they failing?
- Who is winning?
- Why are they winning?
- What are their revenue streams? Profit margins? Capitalization?

- Profit and loss? 10k? Quarterly performance?
- Who is dominating?
- How can I dominate?
- Demographics and Psychographics of my target market?
- How can I continue tightening expenses and liabilities and expanding income and assets?

When you get to the point that you have far more questions than answers and can make effective decisions without always having all the facts, then your adventure is picking up steam. Full speed ahead!

CHAPTER 8

THE TAX MAN

BRIEF HISTORY OF IRS

Origin

The roots of IRS go back to the Civil War when President Lincoln and Congress, in 1862, created the position of commissioner of Internal Revenue and enacted an income tax to pay war expenses. The income tax was repealed 10 years later. Congress revived the income tax in 1894, but the Supreme Court ruled it unconstitutional the following year.

16th Amendment

In 1913, Wyoming ratified the 16th Amendment, providing the three-quarter majority of states necessary to amend the Constitution. The 16th Amendment gave Congress the authority to enact an income tax. That same year, the first Form 1040 appeared after Congress levied a 1 percent tax on net personal incomes above $3,000 with a 6 percent surtax on incomes of more than $500,000.

In 1918, during World War I, the top rate of the income tax rose to 77 percent to help finance the war effort. It dropped sharply in the post-war years, down to 24 percent in 1929, and rose again during the Depression. During World War II, Congress introduced payroll withholding and quarterly tax payment

A New Name
In the 50s, the agency was reorganized to replace a patronage system with career, professional employees. The Bureau of Internal Revenue name was changed to the Internal Revenue Service. Only the IRS commissioner and chief counsel are selected by the president and confirmed by the Senate.

Today's IRS Organization
The IRS Restructuring and Reform Act of 1998 prompted the most comprehensive reorganization and modernization of IRS in nearly half a century. The IRS reorganized itself to closely resemble the private sector model of organizing around customers with similar needs. Source: www.irs.gov

Why did I lead the reader down the path of tax memory lane? It is to drive home the point that whatever we do in healthcare or in business, there will always be a standard to which you are held. In instances where there is not a standard, then seek to set one of the highest caliber possible. Another point that I desire to make crystal clear is, do not mess the tax man! Be respectful and pay all that you owe especially as a corporate entity. The founding fathers of this country were all entrepreneurs and to this day U.S. tax code still favors the wise and judicious operation of legitimate tax shelters as a fundamental driver of free enterprise.

Another point to be contemplated is how nurse entrepreneurs shall position themselves to profitably develop and then standardize a system or process of addressing the greatest challenges to not only the profession of nursing but the healthcare industry?

The following list only scratches the surface of important issues that beg for progressive, forward thinking strategies that whole industries could be created around:

- Workplace bullying
- Emergency preparedness
- Reducing and preventing exposure to biological and airborne hazards
- Workplace violence prevention (patient against staff, patient against patient, patient family against staff, patient family against patient, staff against staff, active shooters, child abductions, identification of sex trafficking victims, etc.)
- Ergonomics
- Lowering and preventing hospital readmissions
- Preparedness and response plans to pandemics and pandemic prevention strategies
- Solutions to finding and qualifying armies of healthcare workers despite attrition due to retirement and escalating time and tuition cost requirements
- Delivering superior quality healthcare to larger sectors of any given community

- Delivering better financial and mental health
  models for addressing burgeoning homeless
  populations everywhere.

I could probably spend months listing pressing issues
screaming for answers. Maybe you have noticed the variety
and quantity of supplies that make their way into any
healthcare setting. Have you stopped to ask yourself, why so
many products marketed in health industry journals are also
marketed in education-based health industry journals? This is
because one day some doctor, nurse or support staff said to
themselves: Why not *my* crazy solution to this ongoing problem? And to this I will add, why not use *my* crazy solutions to
this ongoing dilemma facing your area of expertise?

THE TAX MAN
One thing that I want every employee to understand is that
you owe your jobs existence, description and scope of practice to your employer. Now with that being said, you must
also realize as a nurse or anyone who punches a clock that
your employer sees things differently. They may say that you
are an asset to make you feel warm, fuzzy and valued.

However, on his or her profit and loss statement all employees are a justifiable expense that must be contained.
Nursing always represents the largest fixed overhead cost
anywhere. Don't think that employers have not thought
about replacing us with foreign substitutes that are hungry for
work at a fraction of the hourly rate. The fact that they must
provide insurance and shell out precious capital in the event
of injury. Then there is productivity lost from sickness or

legal expenses due to acts of omission or commission on your part and you can fathom the mounting costs that register in their accounting liability column per employee.

It is not a coincidence that the paid time off column keeps shrinking and that every time annual enrollment comes around you are paying more out of pocket costs for less insurance coverage. I highlight all of this to say, don't be naive! Give your best to your employer AND establish your financial independence post haste!!

From a tax advantage standpoint, employees have relatively few itemized deductions to declare. One eye opener for me was that if you are in a 28% tax bracket, then 28% of your hard-earned dollars are going to the tax man BEFORE you begin to see fiscal daylight!!! In other words, 28% of 365 potential work days is 131 days or 4 months and 11 days worked exclusively paying taxes.

On the other hand, your employer can create numerous corporate tax deductions from properly structured tax shelters. Continuing to work feverishly only to pay out excessive and unnecessary taxes was not what the founding fathers of this country had in mind. Reducing expenses and liabilities along with creating, expanding and preserving personal wealth is every citizen's responsibility. I am merely stressing the need to be properly incorporated in a business or businesses of your own. The corporate tax savings alone, from working in harmony with the tax man, can sometimes equal and potentially even eclipse revenue generated on a quarterly or yearly basis when done properly. Hence, having a shrewd account and tax attorney is indispensable to your wealth building efforts.

CHAPTER 9
THE UNSCRIPTED FUTURE

THE UNSCRIPTED FUTURE
If I attempted to highlight the full spectrum of what nurse entrepreneurs are doing and what can be done, time and space would not permit. Suffice it to say that if you typed nurse entrepreneurs into your favorite search engine, each and every nurse would blow your mind with their talent and untapped potential for great things. Books like *How I became a Nurse Entrepreneur* and nurse organizations like the National Nurses in Business Association (NNBA), National Black Nurses Association (NBNA) and other movements are all very inspiring and indicative of imagination, unity and strength in numbers.

Do you believe that you were meant for great things? Do you have a yearning to answer that adventurous call of the wild?

Or have you done what I did for far too many years? I settled for far less than what my paycheck said my time, my youthful energies and abilities were worth and it was even worse than that. I stopped dreaming about all that was possible, I lost that spark and that desire to know do and be more, I was sleepwalking.

What I saw happening to old nurses in time shook me—Working 35, 40+ years only to join the vast majority of Americans that are alive but barely living. Worse yet they burned up their retirement assets and are still having to work besides mounting health challenges and age discrimination. NO ONE should allow themselves to come to these desperate circumstances and tolerate such humiliation. This is beneath everyone's dignified bearing. If this gets you angry, GOOD! That's 'cause it's time to get fired up and summons the desire for rightly wanting—yes demanding—a better life for yourself and your family.

What will happen in the near future? Who knows? Will nursing schools ever graduate more nurses than are retiring? Will the future nurse entrepreneur require a melding of Master's Degrees to effectively thrive in the marketplace of tomorrow? Will hospitals continue closing faster than they can be built? Will the whole model of healthcare delivery be radically different than our predecessors imagined it? Than we ever imagined it? Or will it merely morph into a new wild western frontier of health service demands capitalized upon by the next generation of nursing millionaires and billionaires in the Age of the Entrepreneur? This is the part of the future script that only you can write…so, make it a great one!!

Author's Note
At first, I had the imagined ending the book here and keeping things short and sweet. Then another thought occurred to

me, why not share just some to the hard lessons that I learned in my own personal attempts at business. Think of all the great nursing mentors and true servant leaders that helped shape your current nursing philosophy. What I loved most about best, most experienced nurses were that they keep things real, the only reason they made it 40, 60,75 years in nursing was that they made the BIG mistakes and lived to tell the tale. I don't imagine that the best, most experienced business leaders came up any differently and have the battle scars to show for it. In the following pages, I decided that instead of painting hypothetical scenarios I would just share some of best entrepreneurial lessons learned from falling flat on my face multiple times in real estate.

Special thanks to real estate brokers Paula Silberberg and Debbie Deeb whose kindness and sincerity towards me as mentors cannot be fully expressed in words. They are champions in business and successes as human beings for which I owe a debt of gratitude.

I also felt it appropriate to include a glossary of key business terms and 25 of my favorite financial books, mentors in written form who I would love to meet someday.

PART 2

12 SURE FIRE WAYS TO FAIL MISERABLY IN YOUR 1ST YEAR AS A REAL ESTATE AGENT

How bad did I Fail my 1st year? I failed so bad that if failure could replace success, I would put on seminars and charge $1,000 per person so people could clamor around me and say, "WOW! How can I be a total failure like you because you are SO NOT the man" The following insights, were one of many of my forays as a nurse into the world of entrepreneurism that met me with brass knuckles and steel toed boots. I had my, you know what, handed back to me. Many will find this part of the book entertaining, at the least, and at most will gain from within these pages my experiences, lumps and bruises that can hopefully soften the blows of hard choices. I don't believe that these failures made me bitter, only better. Learning from failures and growing from it is the foundation upon which great successes are built.

CHAPTER 10
FAILURE #1: NOT REALIZING THAT MAKING A START IN REAL ESTATE IS LIKE LEARNING ANOTHER LANGUAGE.

Learning another language is no joke! People come to America from other countries not knowing a lick of English, live and work here for the next 40 years and guess what? They still did not learn even two new words of English. Why? Because according to professor of linguistics Chris Lonsdale, "Total language immersion per se, is not the answer. Immersing someone in a pool who doesn't know how to swim means they are drowning unless taught in some way to swim." So, one can simply be extracted from that dangerous no win scenario or be introduced slowly and systematically to better tools, systems and training to tip the statistical scales of success of full language mastery in their favor.

Many get into real estate and find that as with any language, it is a whole brained equation. It simultaneously involves numerous skill sets; bodies of knowledge, tribal social dynamics, massive, massive action and the passing of time to move from incomprehensible concepts to relevancy, concrete infancy to abstract mastery. This is a very tall order indeed. In my estimation, this alone contributes to what the national association of realtors has identified as a high failure or burn out rate of real estate agents leaving the industry within their 1st year.

CHAPTER 11

FAILURE #2: NO PROTOCOLS UNIVERSALLY SHARED FOR DEALING WITH CRISES.

As a nurse having worked my entire 22 years in a hospital setting, and knowing what to do even when I didn't know what to do was a comfort. It was a shock to my system to experience one crisis after the next at the local real estate brokerage firm and be totally paralyzed by lack of knowledge and/or lack of how to implement said knowledge. That is why I share my rendition of:

REAL ESTATE EMERGENCY CODES [protocols anyone can enact for unplanned issues, life threatening scenarios]

Code Red: A deal on fire, panic, hysteria or confusion on the part of another agent or potential home buyer/home seller.

Code Blue: Deal is dead or dying quickly despite heroic measures to save it. Like most life and death statistics, no amount of tactics or strategies will save the situation. Someone (this means you) will have to take charge, call it quits, say goodbyes, call for last rites and move on.

Code Pink: effective emergency strategies for preventing violent attempts against agents abducting other agents' clients, contracts, commissions, etc., while deal/ negotiations are still in their infancy.

Code Grey: local, state or federal regulations that make all parties accountable for words and actions.

Strategies and no tolerance policies to deal with disruptive, aggressive, hostile types with and without weapons:

Homeowners and families, homebuyers, seller's agent, buyer's agent, brokers, appraisers, contractors, title companies, banker/lender, etc. Especially, common sense strategies that protect the agent in the office, when out showing homes, and at open houses.

Code Black: Bomb threat or at least potential for an entire market to implode based on unethical behaviors or criminal acts of omission or commission.

Code White: Hostage situation; peoples' finances taken hostage by banker/lender. Fiscal hostilities with FICO scores and increasingly complicated real estate regulations.

Code Yellow: Nationwide economic meltdown, (yet future) when banks and financial establishments will have to close doors indefinitely until root causes of meltdown are identified and apprehended.

Code Orange: Hazardous mentality incident. Many people have toxic dementia/psychosis revolving around money indicative of lack of discipline, irrational fears and inability to focus squarely on issues at hand. A pervasive poverty mentality as I experienced it is typically a prelude to any mass financial crisis.

Code Green: Active disaster plan. This is a business disaster plan for replacing cost to rebuild, present and future revenue lost, key man insurance, manpower, etc.

Code Silver: Active Shooter. Today's work reality must now broaden the list of disaster protocols along with evacuations, extreme weather and fire. Run, hide, fight is one of many active shooter protocols that can be easily added to a risk assessment safety strategy.

CHAPTER 12

FAILURE #3: NOT REALIZING THAT YOU
ARE THE SURGEON IN ANY
REAL ESTATE TRANSACTION.

Too many potential home buyers and sellers treat the real estate agent like a do boy or do girl janitor, thinking they snap
their fingers and agents go fetch. It sure does not work that
way at all! In actuality, it is the Agent that is a surgical consultant who fully and absolutely controls the basis of any
contractual involvement for home sale or purchase. Each patient (the home and home owner) must undergo a full and
thorough diagnostic assessment to ascertain the true nature of
all that is involved and whether the service(s) the surgeon
provides will be an appropriate fit.

The patient is obligated to be as cooperative and forth-
right as possible knowing good and well that it is the surgeon's sole discretion as to if and when they will go "into the
cut" (performing complicated, precision maneuvers necessary
to preserving the financial life of buyer and seller involving
their highest risk financial obligation). Any time people put

themselves out there, that is, seeking to buy or sell, there is a great deal on the line. Also, like all surgeries some have great outcomes and some die on the table. This cannot be helped in some cases as numerous variables drove the outcome such as the physical home's status, the client's financial picture, current market variables, the extent to which one or both parties told the whole truth or conveniently choose not to reveal all facts crucial to an accurate diagnosis and treatment plan, etc. Like the surgeon, many find it so easy and convenient to blame the agent for their own poor choices and outright fiscal irresponsibility. Just keep in mind under these circumstances that it is not a matter of if you will be sued, but when.

CHAPTER 13

FAILURE #4: NOT GRASPING THE UNDERCURRENT OF COMPLEX FINANCIAL PSYCHOLOGY THAT ACCOMPANIES LARGE FINANCIAL TRANSACTIONS OF ANY KIND.

One almost needs to be just as much a real estate psychologist as they are a real estate agent. As with the real estate codes, again, I will utilize a graduated-on site hospital location approach to explain real estate psychological equivalencies that an agent is bound to encounter.

Hospital Sites and Real Estate Psychological Equivalencies:

The Emergency Medical System: typically many utilize this service only when their health and well-being has become desperate and life threatening. Few, if any, notice the "team approach" of a second ambulance arriving at times with police and even fire rescue depending on the nature of the emergency. All of this in an effort to stabilize a patient with numerous health needs and challenges that will be moved along on this assembly line of service providers.

Others drove to the hospital of their "choice" after looking to Dr. Google and social media MD to ascertain the highest performance rating. These will also face the same healthcare dynamics once admitted of a team approach of doctors and nurses, physical, occupational, speech and respiratory therapists, case managers, social workers, etc. Either way that they come into the hospital, a certain percentage have unrealistic expectations of quick fixes that are simply not within the realm of possibility.

The psychological equivalency to real estate is also missed by these same people whose financial health is in crisis, need emergent answers and will still face a team approach to resolution regardless of who Dr. Google directs them to in terms of performance ratings. That team will include real estate brokers, real estate agents, mortgage brokers, title companies, banks, appraisers, contractors, etc. Now that the government has handed down federal regulations regarding financial lending practices the process of home buying and selling takes even longer. Some potential buyers and sellers approach to problem resolution is more the equivalent of bar hopping than sober professional consultancy. They are looking for a one night stand and a good time instead of a serious committed long-term relationship with someone they can take home to mama. I soon found that I hated chasing people down for a contract and now only wanted mutually beneficial relationships with people who respected my time and the skills I brought to the table.

The Emergency Room: What many patients don't want to acknowledge is that their desperate physical condition is no longer under their control and they must accept help that is not on their terms. These individuals are now forced to confront the hard realities of their sickness and, as such, all manner of emotions that crop up; anger, denial, helplessness, embarrassment, fear, with some on the verge of a psychological breakdown at the prospect of death. Then there are the character flaws of pride, lack of self-discipline and self-motivation, immaturity, outright laziness, no social skills, arrogance, hatred of structure and commitment to anyone or anything, unwillingness to make better decisions, lack of respect for themselves and others. (These are the real reasons why things are as they are wouldn't you say?) This is why hospital emergency codes came into existence to deal with patients that kick, bite, punch, spit and in many other ways fight against accepting their own desperate reality and the responsibility to also be a cooperative partner in their own plan of care.

Real estate equivalency makes the brokers office the same as the emergency room with all of the same emotional and psychological baggage in tow. If you can even get the client in the office, their weaknesses and darkest fears, hidden by a tsunami of objections, will reveal itself in a short interview.

The admission to a hospital bed: A journey or process of grieving begins for many who are angry that they are admitted with plenty of denial in tow. This is especially so when they thought the doctor would come and waive his or her stethoscope to and fro and elicit immediate healing and forgiveness for years of poor health choices and now irreversible clinical conditions. Since this did not happen for them there will be plenty of blame to go around.

The real estate equivalency is that now the broker and agent's job is to break both the good and bad news to them. On the one hand yes, there are strategies that can be employed to elicit positive changes in circumstance. On the other hand, there will be no speedy resolution to the economic messes they have made for themselves over the course of decades. So of course it will be the agent's fault that things aren't right because before coming to YOUR office they were in blissful ignorance of just how bad off their financial picture really was with no speedy solutions in sight.

The Intensive care unit: This setting merely intensifies the emotions of the grieving process when the patient and family members involved in decisions about their care must face cold facts. Here in this setting an even wider network of professionals maybe consulted in an attempt to turn dire circumstances around with more complicated approaches to care. It may be the first time all parties are put in touch with just how bad off things really are and now must face tough decisions and choices. No one wants to confront their own mortality, the questions of when is enough, enough? When do we pull the plug? Absolutely frightening and worse yet, there is nowhere to run.

The real estate equivalency is that many who seek real estate services are completely unaware of the grander complex realities that devolve around their serious financial problems. In some cases the situation is not salvageable, especially in cases of insolvency. I find it curious that the negotiation process is engaged in at a "bargaining table", as this is one of the steps in the grieving process. Whether they choose to confront the issue with your broker's office or someone else, in reality there is nowhere to hide. Running away from reality and choosing not to face it is never in anyone's best interests.

The Medical Surgical Floor: This is where most patients are admitted to the hospital from the emergency room with a miscellaneous variety of diagnoses. This is area is just as much a treatment area for the various admission diagnoses as it is a sociological playground of human study. What I am getting at is that here is where bullying, intimidation, manipulation, dishonesty, perversions, lies, vices, racial, cultural, nationalistic, and socioeconomic prejudices, class distinctions, haughtiness, arrogance, ignorance, etc., is revealed. Their expression often driving why people act out the way that they do when vulnerable to illness and in some cases, leave the hospital against medical advice. The health care worker is also exposed and made vulnerable to the human condition. Any who think that these unaccounted for intangibles are not also a driver in why health professional tire of bedside care and ultimately leave, then they may be just as delusional as the psychiatric patient population.

The real estate equivalency is that the ugliest human behaviors rear their head from the beginning to the end of any large financial transaction. Too many agents just do not have the coping skills to deal with these negative human dynamics and have no way to process them and successfully make allowances for them. No doubt about it, it is brutal as bullies and hostilities don't just exist in the hospital setting. It is as raw and unfiltered as the litigation it foments.

The Discharge Plan: When the hospital team has come to the end of all that can be done for the patient, then plans are made for outpatient follow up care if needed. For those who still need extraordinary care, they will be sent to a facility setting that is specific to their short term or long-term rehabilitation needs. At this point, another team will need to assume control of their care. Note I said need, not because the patient wants it but that is what in many cases is absolutely necessary and must practically be accepted. The real estate equivalency is that often what the client wants and what the home and homeowners needs dictate are two radically different things. The markets realities will also dictate hand off to another team of professionals who must rehab the homeowner's expectations as well as address the homes rehab needs to accomplish what must be practically accepted.

CHAPTER 14

FAILURE #5: NOT INVESTING IN BUSINESS SUCCESS COACHING/MENTORING PROGRAMS

This becomes an undeniable necessity whether the broker provides the training or you take it upon yourself to sharpen and hone all the elements of what constitute success. I must say that I had a very positive experience with the Brian Buffini coaching platform. For many who may protest at the cost of continued education, I only have one question to ask. If the education can accelerate you further along toward the fulfillment of your goals or purpose, then how big a price tag can be placed on that? As far as I see it, continued whining over cost says that you don't prize your inalienable right to accomplish as you say you do.

CHAPTER 15

FAILURE #6: NOT IMPLEMENTING SYSTEMS, SYSTEMS, SYSTEMS MAN!

A system by definition is a set of policies and procedures for getting things done or an organized method. If you are not surrounded by, running and improving systems constantly you are:

A. Not in business
B. Wasting mountains of time and energy that could be concentrated at generating profits and expanding your capacity to make even more.
C. Guaranteed to be outpaced in every way, shape and form by fellow agents in the same office and your competitors who don't operate without systems.

When you think of business systems, think of the McDonald's franchise. Having a system for every key activity in place allows teenagers to consistently and effectively run multimillion dollar enterprises. It makes it easy to delegate and duplicate. In other words, systems create massive leverage of time, assets, and resources that allow you to focus on your biggest clearly identifiable income producing activities. Was I outgunned in this area by veteran agents? Absolutely! My ignorance was their glory, my use of too many overly complicated systems was exponentially outpaced by their superior, streamlined systems utilized to maximum effectiveness.

WHAT CAN BE CONSIDERED A BUSINESS SYSTEM?

- It can be a computer or paper database for tracking referrals.
- It can be a paper or electronic form or forms that outline or resolve a problem.
- A scripting system used on the phone or in person that keeps all interactions consistently professional and engaging.
- It can be a list of goals or key activities that spell out the highest daily priorities.
- A daily appointment scheduling system, paper or electronic that allows you to only book people by appointment just like doctors, lawyers and hair stylists. You stay focused and out rightly reject time wasting activities and clients that will suck time and drain your mental and physical energy and waste your monetary resources for lack of structure.
- It can be another person or company that you have delegated to put up brokerage signs in the yard.
- It can be a marketing system (a continuous, never ending, multi-pronged way of acquiring new client

leads converting to more and more commissioned sales and expanding your referral database). This dynamic is pivotal to ALL business conducted anywhere. I will also add that if this is not happening for you are not in business for yourself. You are just in big trouble!!

- Joining an association or chamber of commerce that gives you access to more free or paid for systems mission critical to your business advancement.

- A Business Plan that is practical and actionable with metrics to track business analytics so that you can stay relevant by always KNOWING YOUR NUMBERS. It is only the targets that you consistently hit translates to what will expand your corporate bank account.

- A lead generation system for amassing leads is the process of building a massive referral database. An offline and online lead generation system should preferably have built in system for lead conversion to booked appointments, kept appointments, and finally signed contracts that successfully close.

- Policies and Procedures manual that is either given to you or that you formulate that clearly stipulates what the scope of your roles and functions are necessary to the successful conduct of day to day business operations. Talent recruitment and retention strategies and their scope of practice, accountability, coaching and mentoring programs, rewards systems, business culture or work atmosphere you want to create and even developing teams within teams to achieve specific objectives. Who will hire and fire tied to well defined performance goals, as well as answer who will manage what systems.

- Must also have a system that evaluates and upgrades the current effectiveness and efficiency of all systems in play at present. Do not hesitate to replace mediocre and good systems with great and superior systems that could be the difference maker in transforming the very nature of what can be achieved.

- Effective systems in place will allow people to work systems and you work the systems. Also, superior systems attract superior people and yield superior results.

CHAPTER 16

FAILURE #7: NOT MAKING USE OF OTHER PEOPLE'S_____

I mentioned this list in Part 1 of this book but it is worth repeating:

Aside from OTHER PEOPLE'S MONEY there are:

OTHER PEOPLE'S TIME
OTHER PEOPLE'S RESOURCES
OTHER PEOPLE'S KNOWLEDGE
OTHER PEOPLE'S EXPERIENCES
OTHER PEOPLE'S SKILLSETS
OTHER PEOPLE'S IMAGINATIONS
OTHER PEOPLE'S STRENGTHS
OTHER PEOPLE'S MOTIVATIONS
OTHER PEOPLE'S CHARISMA
OTHER PEOPLE'S LOOKS
OTHER PEOPLE'S INVENTIONS
OTHER PEOPLE'S NETWORKS

OTHER PEOPLE'S DATABASES
OTHER PEOPLE'S SCRIPTS
OTHER PEOPLE'S WEBSITES
OTHER PEOPLE'S BOOKS
OTHER PEOPLE'S BLOGGINGS
OTHER PEOPLE'S MERCHANDISE
OTHER PEOPLE'S SUPERCONNECTIONS
OTHER PEOPLE'S PLATFORMS
OTHER PEOPLE'S REAL ESTATE
OTHER PEOPLE'S MARKETING
OTHER PEOPLE'S MARKET RESEARCH
OTHER PEOPLE'S SYSTEMS
OTHER PEOPLE'S COACHING
OTHER PEOPLE'S WEALTH...

You get the idea that business is also about tapping the creativity, innovation, imagination, etc., of yourself and others. I saw a very cool interview once with famed martial artist Bruce Lee who described his new martial art discipline as being fluid like water which can overcome anything and takes on the shape of whatever it encounters. Bruce Lee developed an expression of martial arts that was personal to him called Jeet Kune Do (JKD). Translated it means, Way of the Intercepting Fist. The arts main tenet: Using no way as way; having no limitation as limitation. The idea of intercepting is key to JKD, whether it be the interception of your opponent's technique or his intent. The basic guiding principles are: simplicity, directness and freedom (the form of no form). The techniques and philosophies of JKD can be applied to real combat as well as challenging life situations (like real estate). Jeet Kune Do consists of physical techniques and applied philosophies and requires the individual to train him or herself to their most cultivated state of being-ness so that when faced with a combat situation or a challenging personal situation, the tools needed are available in the moment and can be executed without thought. I included all this to say the head game of success orientation that you bring to whatever you do is vital to overcoming and transcending current obstacles, problems, and issues.

CHAPTER 17
FAILURE #8: NO REFERRAL DATABASE

This one right here is why you will run crazy like a fox for a time, by not having this in play, once you hang your license under a broker of choice. This is also why you will notice seasoned brokers, broker associates and agents, with expansive referral databases that allows them to set sales records while not seeming to expend much energy at all. I personally encountered agents with databases of 5000 clients or more, yes you read that right. Building a database like this is not impossible unless you make it impossible for yourself. Just know that like anything else worth achieving, this will take time, and an effective daily strategic system for recruitment, retention and expansion. The 80/20 rule applies here, 20% of these clients can yield as much as 80% of your commissioned business! If on a daily basis you continue to consistently refine, upgrade, qualify, initiate reward systems, and build an excellent rapport with your database, then another phenomenon occurs. The 90/10 rule occurs, even the 99/1 rule where a smaller and smaller percentage of clients can yield the vast majority of steady referrals that are ready to buy or sell today!

CHAPTER 18
FAILURE #9: NO TEAMBUILDING

To date, from all the financial seminars attended, books I have read and wealth people that I have spoken to in many fields of endeavor, I have yet to encounter any who achieved millionaire status without a team. The idea of anyone being a self-made millionaire is simply not true. Even if they developed a product or service that almost sells itself, other people still needed to be involved in the process. For real estate, you will need to 1st determine what you and only you can perform at genius level that generates net profits. Then, you must build a team or effectively delegate to and manage talented people who are geniuses themselves at what you cannot do or are unwilling to do.

Almost immediately you must determine, entrepreneurially as a CEO, in what areas can you fire yourself in growing your business? (He with the biggest armies, wins):

- A secretary or administrator that can process paper-work on each contract and make calls that do not require your physical presence.
- A virtual assistant that can perform tasks that are not required on site
- A gopher who can perform low priority, nonprofit producing tasks that otherwise waste focus, time and energy.
- A photographer to take professional pictures of properties you are listing.
- And many more.

Spend less and less time *in* your business, AND more time *on* your business.

CHAPTER 19
FAILURE #10: NOT IT SAVVY

This area is still an embarrassing sticking point for me even though I want to know and do so much more. Technology limitations, both in terms of not having access to the best technological systems and not knowing enough to fully utilize its potential, will be a HUGE competitive disadvantage in an era where you adapt or you die!! It is your entrepreneurial duty to fully capitalize on every tool imaginable in order to perform in ways not previously thought possible. From a global business standpoint, when everything is going digital and transactions that use to take months is happening in fractions of a second! Take every course, read every book, mentor with every computer nerd or software maven imaginable. One thing I refuse to believe is that you can have too much computing power or too many websites. Unlimited thinking and boundless possibilities must be discovered and explored if you are to stretch beyond the crystallized, inflexible thinking of your competitors.

CHAPTER 20

FAILURE #11: NO AWARENESS OF THE VELOCITY OF MONEY

The principle of the velocity of money is simply how fast money changes hands or the speed of financial transactions as one of many determinates of any nation's Gross National Product (GNP) as an indicator of the health of an economy. For example, in many small 3rd world countries, businesses large and small borrow from lenders charging interests rates of 40% or more out of sheer necessity. Most of these businesses cannot afford a long drawn out repayment process so they must, must, must pay off that loan as fast as humanly possible. How? By explosively making as many product sales transactions possible in the least amount of time to immediately pay back that expensive borrowed money. Then they must just as speedily make the same explosive sales so as to have money both to pay themselves and reinvest in the business.

Whole national economies with fast velocities of money transacted are better off fiscally than economies with slow velocities. In the sphere of your own personal economy, how is velocity important to you? The agent #1 who sold 28 homes and nets $80,000/yr. is now capable of leveraging his time, energy and resource in ways that agent #2 who only sold 7 homes and netted $20,000/yr. in the same timeframe cannot. Hence, it is in the interest of all of us to explode the nature and speed at which we can transform business. This now allows you opportunity to do things like: pay to recruit new talent to delegate to, pay to upgrade to superior systems, pay a personal trainer and or business coach to make you better, etc. In summary, real estate agent #1 is now leveraged powerfully to double or triple his personal economy and move thru the business cycle in ways that agent #2 cannot even contemplate much less incorporate.

CHAPTER 21
FAILURE #12: THE HOLODECK EFFECT

Closely tied to the velocity of money is this intangible phenomenon that does not manifest itself unless it is in the presence of accelerative emergence. The only way to describe it is to give an example of something else. One of my favorite episodes of Star Trek: The Next Generation is the episode *The Nth degree.* Here a crewmember is endowed with super human intelligence by an alien probe and when the safety of the crew is threatened he goes into the holodeck room and does the impossible. He gives the ships computer instructions that holographically creates new machines that never existed before to tie into his higher cerebral functions so that HE now becomes a supercomputer and can make mathematical calculations faster in order to avert disaster.

Perhaps one of my greatest frustrations as a new agent was the realization I could not carry out the holodeck effect as I attempted to generate leads and build a database. I was in a catch 22 which is defined as:

"A problematic situation for which the only solution is denied by a circumstance inherent in the problem or by a rule."

So, because I could not find enough leads that converted to any commissioned sales, then I could not capitalize my business to create new systems that would transition me to super productivity. At the same time, I needed those new and superior systems:

- Better scripting and role playing
- Advanced computer skills training
- Continual offline and offline marketing strategies,
- Latest and greatest IT infrastructure
- Ability to effectively delegate low priority functions and grow my own team
- Business coaching
- *...you get the picture*

All working at full capacity that would allow me to now generate a larger pool of qualified leads converting to commissioned sales. This situation drove me to near madness as I did not know how to extract myself from it and no one was incentivized to extend a hand in my behalf. This is probably where many entrepreneurs in general find themselves. The cure is to propel ourselves out of this situation by gathering new knowledge, creating new tactics and strategies and maximizing the holodeck effect of super productive actions.

PART 3

12 _MORE_ SURE FIRE WAYS TO FAIL IN YOUR 1ST YEAR AS A REAL ESTATE AGENT

One thing I have come to value as a nurse over time is being able to act on validated information especially when life or death scenarios are playing out. It is no different in the area of business when it comes to accurate, real time data being the difference between the life and death of your enterprise. I will make the bold assumption that because of the great value garnered from the 1st two volumes that more practical, actionable information is forthcoming. On this note, I hope not to disappoint anyone in any way, so let us begin.

CHAPTER 22

FAILURE #1: NOT OPERATING SIMULTANEOUSLY AS A REAL ESTATE AGENT AND INVESTOR.

This quirk of operational efficiency is a pattern that I first noticed in nursing but in reality it is everywhere in the universe once your eyes have been open to it. With the passing of time I noticed that many nurses who were in the process of obtaining their master's degree as an Advanced Registered Nurse Practitioner (ARNP) were also procuring a Master's in Business Administration (MBA). When asked why they were doing this, they explained that many of the core curriculums for each degree were so similar that with the expenditure of not too much more energy something wonderful happened. Upon graduating with from a dual master's program, these individuals now had the option of several career paths to choose from, thereby, no longer being limited to bedside nursing or just working for another practice. This same liberated status can be yours if you operate simultaneously as BOTH a real estate agent and a real estate investor.

What exactly is a real estate investor? Here is one definition I discovered on the U.S. Securities and Exchange Commission website:

> "A few people may stumble into financial security. But for most people, the only way to attain financial security is to save and invest over a long period of time. You just need to have your money work for you. That's investing. Knowing how to secure your financial well-being is one of the most important things you'll ever need in life. You don't have to be a genius to do it. You just need to know a few basics, form a plan, and be ready to stick to it. There is no guarantee that you'll make money from investments you make. But if you get the facts about saving and investing and follow through with an intelligent plan, you should be able to gain financial security over the years and enjoy the benefits of managing your money. A real estate investor then is one who evaluates the real estate market and purchases property with the intention of building wealth. Real estate investors can purchase residential or commercial property or a combination of both, based on their specific investment objective."

What I appreciate about this definition is that these are real estate activities you will be engaged in as an agent anyway, why not maximize your efficiency and effectiveness because you are already in the game. There are numerous empowering benefits that come from operating from this new elevated frame of mind.

One, when your personally own income generating property, then it removes the desperation factor of getting the sale which unethical customers can sniff out and use against you. It is proper to operate from a financial posture of strength verses palpable weakness that others will sense about you almost immediately. This right here will be a game changer for you, as only a person with strong money management skills (and I would also add, strong self-management skills) is in any real position of power to help those less fortunate.

Two, when you have achieved even a small leveraged position of wealth, now you can operate in ways that have nothing to do with the market. This posture causes YOU to choose who you will do business with on YOUR terms. Now, like every other aspect of your real estate agency, you will also systematize every aspect and process of your professional real estate investing to build long-term wealth. A system of systems is now in full effect.

CHAPTER 23
FAILURE #2: THE BROTHEL PHENOMENON

Just as the universe is full of dark matter, black holes and all manner of yet to be fully explained mysteries, real estate as its own microcosm is no different. This is an attempt to explain some of the bad and ugly agent realities that occurs more than anyone in the business cares to discuss. The Brothel phenomenon is a criminal ideology that thrives in the minds of some potential customers and even agents. When the ideal conditions and people converge, the brothel mindset transmutes to crystallized reality. Again, I don't know why this criminal mindset occurs other than it does. Just as I have not found a plausible explanation as to why men still fantasize about busty female nurses in "super mini" uniforms and stiletto heels who are ready to please!! After 22 years of nursing I have NEVER seen such a thing occur in any health care setting!!!

Brothel-Middle English, worthless fellow, prostitute, from brothen, past participle of brethren to waste away, go to ruin.

Let us now compare the brothel or sex worker industry to the real estate industry and see if commonalities arise.

Brothels: typically run by a madam or criminal kingpin and depending on the state or country comes under some government regulation.
Brokerage house: Run by a broker and comes under local, state and federal regulation.

Brothels: Keep a steady supply of young, pretty women eager to get clients who pay for performance and companionship.
Brokerage house: Young pretty agents, eager to get clients who pay for performance.

Brothels: The dress code is titillating miniskirts, stiletto heels, and peek a boo attire.
Brokerage house: Though warned against in a professional work environment; miniskirts, stiletto heels and peek a boo attire still persists.

Brothels: How many cases of physical/sexual assault and even death at the hands of dangerous, ill-intentioned people go unreported?
Brokerage house: How many cases of "you know what" perpetrated by "you know who" go unreported. This is especially so at open houses where so many agents still showcase homes alone (again despite stern warnings by brokers and police not to do so!!!)

Brothels: Attract all manner of clientele, some friendly some absolutely dangerous, all illicit with no intention of getting caught. Drugs, alcohol and every other illicit vice also come with the territory.

Brokerage house: Don't get me wrong, the real estate industry attracts many, many good, honest and hard-working people who just want a fair shot at making a real success at real estate. Unfortunately, due to its low entry requirements it can and does attract the following:

- Desperados
- Mercenaries
- Identity thieves and other scam artists
- Sex offenders
- Racists
- MMA types adept at violence and intimidation
- And many others

Be VERY watchful for these individuals as agents and potential clients as they will definitely have a negative impact on your ability to conduct honest, ethical business as a real estate professional.

CHAPTER 24
FAILURE #3: NOT BUDGETING FOR THE LEARNING CURVE

I did not know getting into real estate that Masters and even PhD programs online are being offered. The following is by no means an exhaustive list of concentration areas:

- Contract management
- Customer relationship management
- Social media marketing
- Finance and insurance
- People management
- Strategic Planning
- Project management
- Asset and property management
- Commercial real estate investment analysis
- Real estate appraisal and valuation services
- And many others

All of this is to say that like nursing or any other field of expertise, you just cannot know enough about your trade. This was perhaps yet another area I was outgunned in as a new agent. I was the new recruit now having to compete against seasoned warriors, battle-scarred veterans of the trade having survived thru numerous market booms and busts, well networked and a walking library of relevant market research statistics. The only way to overcome these glaring disadvantages is to cerebrally soak yourself with knowledge and surround yourself with others of like purpose.

Now, just as there are numerous nursing certifications that can be obtained to in any specialized area, there are also numerous real estate designations and certifications that can only be obtain by being fully engaged in your craft. I think the following sample certification is very cool:

ALC—Accredited Land Consultant are the recognized experts in land brokerage transactions of five specialized types: (1) farms and ranches; (2) undeveloped tracts of land; (3) transitional and development land; (4) subdivision and wholesaling of lots; and (5) site selection and assemblage of land parcels. Acquire valuable skills through educational offerings leading to the ALC designation.

The ALC designation is awarded to a petitioner that is a member in good standing of the Realtors Land Institute, has 3 or more years of experience as a REALTOR®, successfully complete five RLI Land University core courses and one RLI Land University elective course in Investment Analysis,

Subdivision Development, Agricultural Land, Transitional Land, Tax Ideas with Exchanging and Creative Real Estate, Tax Ideas and Strategies for Selling Real Estate, Site Selection, and Land Planning and Design

ARM yourself with as many of these certifications as possible with the intention of leveling the playing field or die in your ignorance of the grander scheme of things. Don't grumble about the cost of education, instead be rightly disturbed by what not knowing is costing you every moment of every day, developing a PhD mindset of knowing, doing and being more.

CHAPTER 25
FAILURE #4: AGENT NOT DETERMINING
WHAT THEIR NATURE IS

If you are of a farmer nature, then be about tending your farm area. That is a demographic area that you have chosen online and offline to plant seeds of interest in real estate. Here doing your best to optimize the area that you deal in, determined by size, degree of market penetration and type of market specific crop you are planting. Then watering and tilling the soil of why they should trust you versus another agent for their real estate needs. Ultimately, one hopes in time to bear fruitage in the form of commissioned sales, and robust referrals as the seedlings of future sales.

If you are of a nursing nature, then you will be about nurturing caring relationships with individuals in your circle of influence and expanding that sphere of influence to all that would gladly trust you with their financial life and the financial life of their family members and friends. (serious business!)

If you are of a sales shark nature, then others will sense that in your confident presence that we are going to make the deal happen. (You can smell real estate offenders from 5 miles away and eat intimidators and manipulators for breakfast! I totally mean that metaphorically of course!!)

If you are of a psychologist leader nature, you will see the psychosocial dynamics of dealing with and effectively managing people. They then effectively direct people capital so as to bring out the best capabilities in everyone.

If you are of a IT marketing general nature, then you will direct technological infrastructure, social media and website marketing campaigns to their best and highest use. Hence, you will be waging gloriously profitable virtual warfare in intensely competitive combat scenarios.

One can either choose one nature that suites your business personality best or eclectically take the best from each, becoming your own unique incorporated entity. Operating from a nature that does not suite your personal tastes and demeanor can assuredly make real estate activities a chore, one that you will not tolerate for long. Make sure your business plans and daily schedule of operations accounts for this about yourself. Otherwise, people say things like: "real estate just wasn't for me" or "things just didn't feel right."

CHAPTER 26
FAILURE #5: NO STRUCTURE TO YOUR DAY

What time do you get up in the morning? Just YouTube habits of highly successful people and you will discover that the super successful in any field of endeavor have the following shared traits:

- get up anywhere from 3am to 7am every morning!!!
- have a super schedule that accounts for every minute of every day.
- exercise, meditate and in other ways mindfully affirm their priorities and top up physical and mental energies.
- take time to review short and long-range goals and activities to hone and sharpen focus.
- conduct intensive research in their industry every morning.

Do you believe this gives them a category creating competitive advantage in business over others that saunter into the office around 9ish, fire up their computer, scratch their belly, awaken around the 3rd or 4th cup of coffee and let potential clients, emails and office politics dictate their day? Under these circumstances, it will be impossible to gain any momentum in your professional business life if there is no momentum in your personal life. In other words, I made the sobering discovery that YOU are your business!!! If you are disorganized, unmotivated, and lack focus at home, then you will not suddenly transform into an organized, highly moti-vated, money machine in a professional capacity. This will be reflected in the sales targets you reach (assuming you have even set sales targets for yourself and daily analytics that measure if one is either close to or far from hitting these numbers).

CHAPTER 27
FAILURE #6: NOT HAVING YOUR FINANCIAL AFFAIRS IN ORDER

If your credit cards are maxed out are you really in the best financial position to help others? Do you have a pool of growing assets that allow you to meet the definition of wealth? or are you on the way to out of control debt leading to eminent poverty? Many an agent has crashed and burned money wise long, long before some external market down turn. The seasoned nurse has over time come to terms with the fact that they do not have all the answers nor all the knowledge and do not need to. Shrewdness lies in knowing who on the team to go to as a resource. It is this humble realization that makes good nurses great. The wise seasoned agent has also applied the following "humble teams" approach to money matters and regularly seeks advisement from a growing team of financial professionals: financial advisors, accountants, bankers, lenders and estate planning and real estate attorneys.

- A Financial advisor who can help funnel disciplined dollars into expanding brokerage accounts of pooling assets and facilitate exciting conversations about wealth management and business successes resulting in and from multiple streams of income.

- An accountant worth their salt who can help them with the necessary bookkeeping and fiscal focus of generating weekly personal and business financial statements which is the basis for meaningful discussions about expanding net worth.

- A friendly neighborhood banker that can help them grow at least six months to a year of cash reserves to cover expenses. Personal and business expenses in personal and corporate accounts respectively being absolutely pivotal to sustained fiscal energy required to launch your real estate agency and ramp up your business.

- Attorney's that can help them navigate the increasingly complex and litigious financial landscape and conduct business as safely and cautiously as possible.

CHAPTER 28
FAILURE #7: NOT HAVING A
LONG-TERM PERSPECTIVE

What is your ultimate intention for the pursuit of real estate interests? Is it just to get in and make a bunch of money because everyone else is?

Entertaining such fantasies only reveals a gold rush mentality. What I mean by this is that gold rushes, historically, had very poor outcomes for the majority. If you noticed in every American western movie, the town formed was usually as a result of gold prospectors seeking instant riches.

The only ones that really made the vast fortunes were the ones shrewd and calculated enough to provide the picks, shovels, loose women and gut rot whiskey. What was just as interesting was that when these boom towns went bust, the business men with a long-term perspective were working on other opportunities that expanded their means. Meanwhile, the vast majority of people either went belly up or disappeared. They went chasing the next gold rush, never planting roots long enough to realize the fruitage of anything meaningful. Just talk to some of the real estate agents and brokers who have prospered at their craft after 20 years, 30 years, even 40 plus years of experience!! I love hearing their stories of tragedy and triumphs as the cost of achieving mastery.

CHAPTER 29

FAILURE #8: NOT EFFECTIVELY DEALING WITH IN YOUR FACE PREJUDICE

In my attempt at full disclosure and transparency surrounding the massive success of my failures, I deem it only appropriate to give fair warning of prejudice in all its ugly forms.

Racial bias:
People are not too complicated in this area, they will convey this shortcoming to you in subtle and not so subtle ways. Bottom line?

Even though our country may be a supposed melting pot of races, cultures and beliefs, people still only like and identify with their own kind. East Indian clients prefer only to deal with other East Indian agents and brokers and so forth. This is a cold, quirky reality of any industry. I have encountered people who will not purchase a Cuban sandwich unless it has been prepared in the kitchen by real Cubans!

Gender bias:

Other people are partial to dealing only with like gender. If you happen to find yourself in a brokerage office or area dominated by female agents, for example, then that is the expectation that many will have. As a result, some will feel apprehensive about doing business with a male agent. Still others will deem it inappropriate to deal with anyone but a male agent. I never said that there is any logic involved when it comes to bias.

Age bias:

One thing I quickly grew tired of as a new nurse was the patients young and old that told me I was "too young" to be a nurse! Some even asked to see my driver's license to make sure I was old enough to be practicing. Still others wanted to know if I had graduated high school 1st. An a few out rightly rejected me solely on age and asked for an older nurse as, according to these age authoritarians, I was just too young to possibly know what I was doing!!!! It doesn't get better in real estate where individuals simply will not entrust their biggest financial concerns to someone they feel does not have the assumed competency that they feel must come with the passing of time. Age bias also works at the other end of the age spectrum with some feeling that if you are too old and gray you simply can't keep up or stay relevant regardless of massive expertise and experience.

Experience bias:

Closely related to age bias, some clients will come to your broker and ask to only deal with the most experienced agent available.

Beauty bias:
Certain clientele won't even entertain the thought of dealing
with an agent that is not young and pretty with plenty of sex
appeal. (I didn't say bias was or is in any way appropriate or
relative to delivery of real estate services). This has given
older agents in the industry a complex about looks, hair col-
oring and style of dress.

Location bias:
Potential clients may only want to do business if you are, let's
say, from Philadelphia and love baseball!

Postural bias:
What I mean by this is that some customers only want someone they can manipulate and dominate over in the negotiation process versus the assertive surgeon type who is
eminently in command of every aspect of the relationship.

I want every agent to be aware that these very real biases
exist and better yet, engineer systems, processes and methods
that will work in your favor and not against you.

CHAPTER 30

FAILURE #9: NOT BEING WITH THE RIGHT BROKERAGE OFFICE

As time went on I saw that the office culture or accepted way that daily business was conducted quickly became a limiting factor in the degree of success one could hope to attain. One that can package all necessary elements that will give you the biggest and best leveraged bang for your buck. Another item that is pivotal to your success is asking better questions that lead to getting better answers. The following is by no means an exhaustive list of questions (the questions I did not know to ask) when shopping for the right broker to grow your business under:

- What is their attitude about growth?
- Will I have to generate my own leads? If not, then where will leads come from?
- What are the various lead generation strategies employed in house and what is their conversion to closed deals?

- Do I get to create my own business plan or is there a shared mission, vision and business plan for the brokerage culture?
- How many agents can your office hold?
- Is physical office space a limiting factor in potential future growth?
- Do you even want growth or do things need to stay the way it has always been?
- What are the potential farm areas locally that are yet to be capitalized upon?
- What are the certifications that your office requires that are unique to staying relevant to market demands?
- What is your unique selling proposition that positions you distinctly from the 40 other brokerage offices in town?
- What will be my unique selling proposition that will have clients lining up at my door and filling my voice mail box?
- Do you have a lead researcher or lead generation platform that will scrub leads that are primed for buy or selling homes today?
- To what extent do you work to develop relationships with customers, investors, landlords and hedge fund managers locally, nationally and internationally?
- What marketing materials are available? Do you have preferred vendors who offer products and services?
- If I am selling or buying my own property, what office/franchise fees are required or forgiven? Is there

a limit to the number of residential or commercial properties I can buy or sell in a year?

- What is your commission structure? Commission split for beginners? Does the split rise with increases in my production?

- How do you communicate information to your associates? Sales meetings? Emails? Texts? Websites? Mail slots in office?

- Do you pay any of my startup costs like business cards, signs, name riders, advertising announcements?

- Do you have an application fee to join your brokerage? What does it cover? What will my monthly fees be and/or cover? Examples: copier costs, faxes, scans, transaction fees, errors and omissions insurance.

- What training is offered? Start-up? On-going?

- Do their support personnel in the office (transaction coordinators) assist me? Do I pay a fee for their services? Does your office have computers on site I can use? Does your office have Wi-Fi?

- If this is a national franchise brokerage, what is the franchise fee? How/when is it paid? What is the broker's or franchise's presence on the internet?

- Do you have multiple offices and do I have access to them? Do I office out of my home? What is the cost (if any) of having an office here in your office?

- How many agents do you have and will you share what your total office production was last year? (The 80/20 rule always applies: 20% of the agents in any office will generate 80% of the sales)

CHAPTER 31

FAILURE #10: NO FORMAT FOR THE CONTINUED EXPANSION AND IMPLEMENTATION OF KNOWLEDGE

Nurses and real estate agents are living in an age beyond being just knowledge workers. Now I believe the more appropriate term is not Information Age, it is Implementation Age! The sheer speed at which global business is moving staggering and as such your capacity to both gather relevant information and immediately implement it into an expanding array of monetized product and service offerings is the crux of the matter. Can I do it? If not, who can implement? How fast? How much? And how quick is my return on investment (ROI)?

CHAPTER 32

FAILURE #11: NOT HYPER SPECIALIZING IN AN AREA THAT YOU CAN DOMINATE

Nurses and doctors that specialize are capable of more than those who do not. As your awareness and movement toward mastery of real estate principles progresses you will note that those who focus uniquely on one area of real estate also flourish. Dominance at the one thing done better than anyone else at all times and in all ways places one in their own category were soon you can dictate your own price and terms of engagement. One day just do a search on high performing individuals in any industry and notice the huge jumps in salary, net worth and recognition. This is a very sweet spot to be in and worth the concentrated effort to attain.

CHAPTER 33

FAILURE #12: NOT WORKING HARD
ENOUGH TO HIT YOUR NUMBERS

One of my favorite business books of all time is the 10x Rule
by Grant Cardone. (Buy it, read it, then buy all the rest of his
books to read and re-read till you comprehend the magnitude
of the principles outlined) I felt hugely impacted in my
mindset and focus about the sustained pace and energy that
must be brought to EVERYTHING that one strives to
achieve success in. Mr. Cardone spends a lot of time convey-
ing the total rethink on work and effort times by 10 that will
be required to actually accomplish what was conceptualized.
This area is probably the cemetery for most failures, not just
in real estate or nursing but in life in general. Be clear on the
fact that you are not entitled to success in a free market
economy and no one owes you anything. The whole point of
a free market system is to create an unfair advantage! So the
appropriate question to ask is just how hungry are you? Or
just how serious of a commitment have you made to yourself
and your family that you will do all that you have set your

mind to ascend to the throne? Eminent and well respected real estate coach Brian Buffini calls this state of steady achievement a "peak producer state." As I understand him, it is a purposeful state of financial, physical, mental and spiritual convergence that one grows to causing him to transcend all external obstacles to success by any measure. Hitting sales numbers and exceeding them again and again will be merely an external confirmation of inner transformations. According to Tony Robbins, the inner giant, at this point, has awoken from its long slumber and emerges hungering only for the taste of sweet victory... So feed it.

SOURCE REFERENCES

Preface
Rural Hospitals In Critical Condition USA TODAY 2014/11/12
Bureau of Labor Statistics, U.S. Department of Labor,
Occupational Outlook Handbook, 2016-17 Edition,
Registered Nurses

Part 1
https://www.Businessdictionary.com
https://etymonline.com/index.php?term=entrepreneur
https://mises.org/library/jean-baptiste-say-neglected-
champion-laissez-faire-0
www.AMIA.org
https://www.irs.gov/uac/brief-history-of-irs

Part 2
VDYoutube - How to learn any language in six months |
Chris Lonsdale | TEDxLingnanUniversity
https://www.buffiniandcompany.com/default.aspx
https://bruceleefoundation.org/contact/faqs/

http://www.businessdictionary.com/definition/velocity-of-money.html
https://www.merriam-webster.com/dictionary/catch-22

Part 3

https://www.investor.gov/introduction-investing
http://www.businessdictionary.com/definition/real-estate-investor.html
https://www.merriam-webster.com/dictionary/brothel
https://www.nar.realtor/designations-and-certifications/alc

ABOUT THE AUTHOR

Robert C. Saunders has been a nurse in the Tampa Bay area for over 20 yrs. and is still expanding his horizons as a poet, author, songwriter, entrepreneur, marketer, and any other opportunities blown his way by winds of change.

GLOSSARY OF BUSINESS TERMS BY CHAPTER

In the past, I have gotten into a lot of trouble using certain words and just assuming that the other party must know what I was talking about since I was speaking perfect penguin. The following definitions gleaned are part of my ongoing effort to communicate more clearly so as to prevent misunderstanding.

Chapter 1

Corporation - Etymology from Late Latin *corporatio* ("assumption of a body"), from Latin *corporare*, past participle *corporatus* ("to form into a body").

A group of individuals, created by law or under authority of law, having a continuous existence independent of the existences of its members, and powers and liabilities distinct from those of its members.

Source: *Webster's New International Dictionary of the English Language*, 1909, is a public domain dictionary, as is also the revised 1913 edition.

Market Share - A percentage of total sales volume in a market captured by a brand, product, or company.

http://www.businessdictionary.com/definition/market-share.html

Revenue - The income generated from sale of goods or service, or any other use of capital or assets, associated with the main operations of an organization before any costs or expenses are deducted. Revenue is shown usually as the top item in an income (profit and loss) statement from which all charges, costs, and expenses are subtracted to arrive at net income. Also called sales, or (in the UK) turnover.

http://www.businessdictionary.com/definition/revenue.html

Limited Liability Company - Relatively recent type of US business structure that combines the limited personal liability feature of a corporation with the single taxation feature of a partnership or sole-proprietorship firm. Its profits and tax benefits are split any way the stockholders/ shareholders (whether individuals or other firms) choose. Tax return for a LLC is filed with the taxation authorities only for the purpose of information, and each shareholder files own tax return separately. Also called company limited by share.

http://www.businessdictionary.com/definition/limited-liability-company-LLC.html

Leadership - A leader's singular job is to get results. But even with all the leadership training programs and "expert" advice available, effective leadership still eludes many people and organizations. One reason, says Daniel Goleman, is that such experts offer advice based on inference, experience, and instinct, not on quantitative data. Now, drawing on research of more than 3,000 executives, Goleman explores which precise leadership behaviors yield positive results. He outlines six distinct leadership styles, each one springing from different components of emotional intelligence. Each style has a distinct effect on the working atmosphere of a company, division, or team, and, in turn, on its financial performance. The styles, by name and brief description alone, will resonate with anyone who leads, is led, or, as is the case with most of us, does both. Coercive leaders demand immediate compliance. Authoritative leaders mobilize people toward a vision. Affiliative leaders create emotional bonds and harmony. Democratic leaders build consensus through participation. Pacesetting leaders expect excellence and self-direction. And coaching leaders develop people for the future. The research indicates that leaders who get the best results don't rely on just one leadership style; they use most of the styles in any given week. Goleman details the types of business situations each style is best suited for, and he explains how leaders who lack one or more styles can expand their repertories. He maintains that which practice leaders can switch among leadership styles to produce powerful results, thus turning the art of leadership into a science.

https://hbr.org/2000/03/leadership-that-gets-results

Chapter 2

Return on Investment(ROI) - The earning power of assets measured as the ratio of the net income (profit less depreciation) to the average capital employed (or equity capital) in a company or project. Expressed usually as a percentage, return on investment is a measure of profitability that indicates whether or not a company is using its resources in an efficient manner. For example, if the long-term return on investment of a company is lower than its cost-of-capital, then the company will be better off by liquidating its assets and depositing the proceeds in a bank. Also called rate of return, or yield.

http://www.businessdictionary.com/definition/return-on-investment-ROI.html

Customer relationship management (CRM)

1. A management philosophy according to which a company's goals can be best achieved through identification and satisfaction of the customers' stated and unstated needs and wants.
2. A computerized system for identifying, targeting, acquiring, and retaining the best mix of customers. Customer relationship management helps in profiling prospects, understanding their needs, and in building relationships with them by providing the most suitable products and enhanced customer service. It integrates back and front office systems to create a database of customer contacts, purchases, and technical support, among other things. This database helps

the company in presenting a unified face to its customers, and improves the quality of the relationship,
while enabling customers to manage some information on their own.

http://www.businessdictionary.com/definition/customer-
relationship-management-CRM.html

Scalable - In recent years, scale has become a factor of increasing importance in the design of distributed systems. The
scale of a system has three dimensions: numerical, geographical, and administrative. The numerical dimension consists of
the number of users of the system, and the number of objects
and services encompassed. The geographical dimension consists of the distance over which the system is scattered. The
administrative dimension consists of the number of organizations that exert control over pieces of the system. The three
dimensions of scale affect distributed systems in many ways.
Among the affected components are naming, authentication,
authorization, accounting, communication, the use of remote
resources, and the mechanisms by which users view the system. Scale affects reliability: as a system scales numerically,
the likelihood that some host will be down increases; as it
scales geographically, the likelihood that all hosts can communicate will decrease.

http://citeseerx.ist.psu.edu/viewdoc/summary?doi=10.1.1.31
.3576

Chapter 3

Business unit - A logical element or segment of a company (such as accounting, production, marketing) representing a specific business function, and a definite place on the organizational chart, under the domain of a manager. Also called department, division, or a functional area.

http://www.businessdictionary.com/definition/business-unit.html

Shared service - Shared services have widely spread in the government and private sectors as an alternative to outsourcing. Unlike outsourcing, shared service is the standardization and consolidation of common functions across the multiple organizations to reduce operational cost and to increase information and knowledge sharing. One critical aspect to successful shared services is to maintain specified service levels and response times for each individual organization.

http://citeseerx.ist.psu.edu/viewdoc/summary?doi=10.1.1.53 3.7642&rank=1

Spinoff - Corporate divestiture accomplished through (1) separation of a division or subsidiary from its parent firm to create a new corporate entity by issuing new shares. These shares are distributed to the current stockholders (shareholders) in proportion to their current shareholdings, and may also be sold to the public, or (2) a leveraged buyout by the management of the division or subsidiary.

http://www.businessdictionary.com/definition/spinoff.html

Chapter 4

Management Information Systems - An organized approach to the study of the information needs of an organization's management at every level in making operational, tactical, and strategic decisions. Its objective is to design and implement procedures, processes, and routines that provide suitably detailed reports in an accurate, consistent and timely manner. In a management information system modern, computerized systems continuously gather relevant data both from inside and outside an organization. This data is then processed, integrated, and stored in a centralized database (or data warehouse) where it is constantly updated and made available to all who have the authority to access it, in a form that suits their purpose.

http://www.businessdictionary.com/definition/management
-information-system-MIS.html

Chief information officer (CIO) - Executive responsible for development, implementation, and operation of a firm's information technology policy. He or she oversees all information systems infrastructure within the organization, and is responsible for establishing information related standards to facilitate management control over all corporate resources.

http://www.businessdictionary.com/definition/chief-infor-
mation-officer-CIO.html

Chief financial officer (CFO) - Senior most executive responsible for financial control and planning of a firm or project. He or she is in charge of all accounting functions including (1) credit control, (2) preparing budgets and financial statements, (3) coordinating financing and fund raising, (4) monitoring expenditure and liquidity, (5) managing investment and taxation issues, (6) reporting financial performance to the board, and (7) providing timely financial data to the CEO. Also called chief finance officer, comptroller, controller or finance controller.

http://www.businessdictionary.com/definition/chief-financial-officer-CFO.html

Chief procurement officer (CPO) - Executive level employee of an organization whose responsibilities include sourcing, supply management and procurement for the company. Generally, the CPO reports directly to the CEO of a company.

http://www.businessdictionary.com/definition/Chief-Procurement-Officer-CPO.html

Chief operating officer (COO) - An executive responsible for (1) the day-to-day running of the critical departments of an organization such as production, marketing and sales, and distribution, (2) establishing procedures and processes to ensure their smooth functioning, and (3) providing timely operational information and assistance to the CEO.

http://www.businessdictionary.com/definition/chief-operating-officer-COO.html

Chief marketing officer (CMO) - The company executive responsible for corporate branding, advertising, marketing channels, customer outreach and all other marketing aspects. The CMO is considered part of the top management tier with responsibilities which generally cross all company product lines and geographic regions.

http://www.businessdictionary.com/definition/chief-marketing-officer-CMO.html

Chief knowledge officer (CKO) - Executive responsible for making available the knowledge appropriate to the firm's requirements and strategically important in achieving its goals. He or she (1) administers corporate knowledge as an ongoing and critically valuable resource. (2) is responsible for converting the firm's intellectual property into revenue generating assets, and (3) guides the firm towards becoming (or continuing to be) a learning organization. Also called chief learning officer.

http://www.businessdictionary.com/definition/chief-knowledge-officer-CKO.html

Search engine optimization (SEO) - Refers to the process of improving traffic to a given website by increasing the site's visibility in search engine results. Websites improve search engine optimization by improving content, making sure that the pages are able to be indexed correctly, and ensuring that the content is unique. Going through the search engine optimization process typically leads to more traffic for the site because the site will appear higher in search results for information that pertains to the site's offerings.

http://www.businessdictionary.com/definition/search-engine-optimization.html

Chapter 5

Key person insurance - Key man insurance is simply life insurance on the key person in a business. In a small business, this is usually the owner, the founders or perhaps a key employee or two. These are the people who are crucial to a business--the ones whose absence would sink the company. You need key man insurance on those people. Here's how key man insurance works: A company purchases a life insurance policy on the key employee, pays the premiums and is the beneficiary of the policy. If that person unexpectedly dies, the company receives the insurance payoff. The reason this coverage is important is because the death of a key person in a small company often causes the immediate death of that company. The purpose of key man insurance is to help the company survive the blow of losing the person who makes the business work. The company can use the insurance proceeds for expenses until it can find a replacement person, or, if necessary, pay off debts, distribute money to investors, pay severance to employees and close the business down in an orderly manner. In a tragic situation, key man insurance gives the company some options other than immediate bankruptcy.

If the company is just you and doesn't have any employees or other people who depend on it, then key man insurance isn't as necessary. You'll notice that I didn't mention your family-- don't confuse key man insurance with personal life insurance. If you have a spouse and/or children who depend on your income, then you should have personal life insurance for that purpose.

How do you determine who needs this insurance? Look at your business and think about who is irreplaceable in the short term. In many small businesses, it is the founder who holds the company together--he may keep the books, manage the employees, handle the key customers and so on. If that person is gone, the business pretty much stops.

How much key man insurance do you need? That depends on your business, but in general you should get as much as you can afford. Shop around and get rates from several different agents; most life insurance agents will sell you a key man policy. Be sure to ask for term insurance--many agents will push whole or variable life, which have much higher premiums and commissions but are unnecessary for a key man policy. Ask for quotes on $100,000, $250,000, $500,000, $750,000 and $1 million and compare the costs of each. Then think of how much money your business would need to survive until it could replace the key person, come up to speed and get the business back on its feet. Buy a policy that fits into your budget and will address your short-term cash needs in case of tragedy.

https://www.entrepreneur.com/article/56068

Chapter 6

Leverage - (Author's comment: when I referred to other people's money, time, etc., this is the underlying additive and multiplicative principle to be applied entrepreneurially in unending permutations.) The ability to influence a system or an environment in a way that multiplies the outcome of one's efforts without a corresponding increase in the consumption of resources. In other words, leverage is the advantageous condition of having a relatively small amount of cost yield a relatively high level of returns.

http://www.businessdictionary.com/definition/leverage.html

Barter - Trading in which goods or services are exchanged without the use of cash. Resorted-to usually in times of high inflation or tight money, barter is now a common form of trading in deals such as offers to buy surplus goods in exchange for advertising space or time. Advent of internet has transformed bartering from largely person-to-person to mainly business-to-business exchange where items ranging from manufacturing capacity to steel and paper are bartered across international borders on a daily basis.

http://www.businessdictionary.com/definition/barter.html

Chapter 7

Demography - Study of both quantitative and qualitative aspects of human population. Quantitative aspects include composition, density, distribution, growth, movement, size, and structure of the population. Qualitative aspects are the sociological factors such as education quality, crime, development, diet and nutrition, race, social class, wealth, well-being.

http://www.businessdictionary.com/definition/demography. html

Psychographics - Analysis of consumer lifestyles to create a detailed customer profile. Market researchers conduct psychographic research by asking consumers to agree or disagree with activities, interests, and opinions statements. Results of this exercise are combined with geographic (place of work or residence) and demographic (age, education, occupation, etc.) characteristics to develop a more 'lifelike' portrait of the targeted consumer segment.

http://www.businessdictionary.com/definition/psycho-graphics.html

Market capitalization

1. On-going market valuation of a public firm (whose shares are publicly traded) computed by multiplying the number of outstanding shares (held by the shareholders) with the current per share market price. It is, however, not necessarily the price a buyer would pay for the entire firm. And is not a realistic estimate of the firm's actual size, because a share's market price is based on trading in only a fraction of the firm's total outstanding shares.

2. Sum of the current market value of all securities traded on a financial market.

http://www.businessdictionary.com/definition/market-capitalization-market-cap.html

Peter Ferdinand Drucker - A writer and management consultant who is considered to be the person who invented management and nicknamed the "Father of Modern Management". He is known for writing about business management and how humans are organized within these environments. He first stated in the 1950s that employees were to be considered as assets to a company and not liabilities. Drucker was born in Austria in 1909 and died just days shy of his 96th birthday in 2005.

http://www.businessdictionary.com/definition/Peter-Drucker.html

Famous Drucker Quote

> "This defines entrepreneur and entrepreneurship - the entrepreneur always searches for change, responds to it, and exploits it as an opportunity."

> Source: Drucker, P.F. (2015). Innovation and entrepreneurship practice and principles. London: Routledge.

Profit Margin - Ratio of profit after taxes to cost-of-sales, often expressed as a percentage. It is one of the measures of the profitability of a firm, and an indicator of its cost structure.

Formula: After-tax profit x 100 ÷ cost of sales.

http://www.businessdictionary.com/definition/profit-margin.html

Income statement - A summary of a management's performance as reflected in the profitability (or lack of it) of an organization over a certain period. It itemizes the revenues and expenses of past that led to the current profit or loss, and indicates what may be done to improve the results. In contrast to a balance sheet, an income statement depicts what happened over a month, quarter, or year. It is based on a fundamental accounting equation (Income = Revenue - Expenses) and shows the rate at which the owner's equity is changing for better or worse. Along with balance sheet and cash flow statement it forms the basic set of financial information required to manage an organization.

http://www.businessdictionary.com/definition/income-statement.html

Form 10-K - The federal securities laws require public companies to disclose information on an ongoing basis. For example, domestic companies must submit annual reports on Form 10-K, quarterly reports on Form 10-Q and current reports on Form 8-k for a number of specified events and must comply with a variety of other disclosure requirements.

The annual report on Form 10-K provides a comprehensive overview of the company's business and financial condition and includes audited financial statements. Although similarly named, the annual report on Form 10-K is distinct from the "annual report to shareholders," which a company must send to its shareholders when it holds an annual meeting to elect directors.

Following are the deadlines for companies to file Forms 10-K and 10-Q:

Category of Filer (public float)	Revised Deadlines For Filing Periodic Reports	
	Form 10-K Deadline	Form 10-Q Deadline
Large Accelerated Filer ($700MM or more)	60 days	40 days
Accelerated Filer ($75MM or more and less than $700MM)	75 days	40 days
Non-accelerated Filer (less than $75MM)	90 days	45 days

To find a particular company's Form 10-K filings, use the Company Search for the SEC's EDGAR database. On the returned listing of filings for the company, enter "10-K" in the Filing Type box near the top of the page to filter for only Forms 10-K that have been filed.

Issuers with questions concerning Form 10-K should consult with counsel or contact the SEC's Division of Corporation Finance.

https://www.sec.gov/fast-answers/answers-form10khtm.html

Chapter 8

Balance sheet - A condensed statement that shows the financial position of an entity on a specified date (usually the last day of an accounting period). Among other items of information, a balance sheet states (1) what assets the entity owns, (2) how it paid for them, (3) what it owes (its liabilities), and (4) what is the amount left after satisfying the liabilities. Balance sheet data is based on a fundamental accounting equation (assets = liabilities + owners' equity), and is classified under subheadings such as current assets, fixed assets, current liabilities, long-term Liabilities. With income statement and cash flow statement, it comprises the set of documents indispensable in running a business.

An audited balance sheet is often demanded by investors, lenders, suppliers, and taxation authorities; and is usually required by law. To be considered valid, a balance sheet must give a true and fair view of an organization's state of affairs, and must follow the provisions of GAAP in its preparation.

Also called statement of condition, statement of financial
condition, or statement of financial position.

http://www.businessdictionary.com/definition/balance-
sheet.html

Overhead

1. Resource consumed or lost in completing a process, that does not contribute directly to the end-
product. Also called burden cost.

2. Accounting: A cost or expense (such as for administration, insurance, rent, and utility charges) that
(1) relates to an operation or the company as a
whole, (2) does not become an integral part of a
good or service (unlike raw material or direct labor),
and (3) cannot be applied or traced to any specific
unit of output. Overheads are indirect costs.

3. Data communications: Data bits added to user-
transmitted data, for carrying routing information
and error correcting and operational instructions.

4. Utilities: Energy or water lost during delivery from
the generating or production plant to the end user.

http://www.businessdictionary.com/definition/overhead.ht
ml

Chapter 9

Script

1. to prepare a script for or from

2. to provide carefully considered details for (such as a plan of action) an event carefully scripted to attract attention

Unscripted - not written or planned at an earlier time.

Synonyms: Unplanned, unrehearsed, unexpected, spontaneous, unprepared for, improvised.

https://www.merriam-webster.com/

Recommended Reading
25 recommended books that continue to
shape my financial philosophy

1.   *Think and Grow Rich,* by Napoleon Hill. Even though this book was written in 1937, I believe that the wealth principles distilled in this seminal work can and does have a transformational effect on each individual's capacity to look at old problems in a solution oriented way. The late great Jim Rohn once observed that poverty in and of itself is not the problem. The problem is that there is a poverty of thoughts, a massive shortage of wealth building ideas that could be applied to fundamentally lifting each of us to a new state of living and being. At least that is what I understand his words to mean. This book has affected some to such a degree that they read it daily, not wanting to miss one efficacious morsel.

2.   *The Richest Man in Babylon,* by George Samuel Clason. Despite the setting for this collection of parables taking place in ancient Babylon, these lessons in financial wisdom could just as easily have been written yesterday. The principles outlined are so simple and so profound that I have lost count of how many times I have listened to the audio

book for its sheer practicality and insights. Something new that I learned about this book was that it was originally a series of separate informational pamphlets distributed by banks and insurance companies. Eventually, the pamphlets were bound together and published in book form in 1926. For some reason, I can't stop geeking out about this as I find that factoid to be very cool.

3.   *Poor Charlie's Almanack: The Wit and Wisdom of Charles T. Munger.* For those who may be unfamiliar with Mr. Munger, you may now his investment partner and lifelong friend Warren Buffet. I must fairly warn you that this book is a Juggernaut of insights that he has gathered from a lifetime of voracious reading and astute observations. What is more, he takes the reader thru the museum of his mind and experiences compiled in a way that one rarely would experience elsewhere. In my estimation, the pinnacle of his achievement is what he seeks to leave us all with. That being the embodiment of his legacy, a series non-emotional, distilled mental models that will allow one to theoretically strip down any touted investment and hyper analyze its validity. If at the end of the assembly line of this caustic process, that investment is sound and still standing on its own merits, then and only then will that investment have any merit worth pursuing. It is no wonder that out of the thousands of investments that came across their table at Berkshire Hathaway, so few made the final cut. I often ponder how many of us would have been spared so much financial pain in the stock market, in real estate, in business, etc., if we could

just remove emotion and herd mentality from our day to day
financial decisions.

4.   *Multiple Streams of Income: How to generate a
lifetime of unlimited wealth,* by **Robert G. Allen.** I can't
believe this book was published in 2000 and I still find the
gems in this masterpiece just as fresh and compelling as when
I read it the 1ˢᵗ time. What is tragic is how slow I was and still
am in absorbing these principles. I had to experience foreclo-
sures and bankruptcy in my own personal economy even before the real estate market came crashing down, in order to
finally get what Mr. Allen was even talking about. A big take
away for me, is that it is not enough just to read books once
and intellectualize it. No, no! I watched wealth guru Tia
Lopez in a TED Talk explain what he meant by reading a
book a day. What he advocates is touching the same set of
books over and over and over again until the knowledge from
these books makes a transactional change in your health, your
relationships, and the wealth in your bank account.(Actively
seeking out success mentors who wrote these books and
hounding them till they help pull you up is also helpful) According to Mr. Allen, it is our duty in the land of opportunity
to create as many streams and aggregate pools of income as
necessary to create a lifetime of prosperity for yourself that
allows one to be congruent with their life purpose. Don't
over complicate these methodologies, merely start where you
are and concentrate your mental powers upon building one
stream at a time.

5.   ***Speak to Win*, by Brian Tracy.** In actuality, every single book that this international motivational speaker and success trainer has ever written is worth reading over and over. A most excellent point made in this book is that learning to speak in front of audiences and communicating your vision well is unavoidable to your future success. Hence, it is in your unequivocal best interest to prepare to master the art of speaking. Prepare and practice over and over again for months and years to come, no shortcuts to having the life that you desire. Mr. Tracy doesn't leave you in the dark. He has distilled the principles he learned in the trenches from having given thousands of speeches over the last 40 plus years.

6.   ***The World is Flat: A Brief history of the Twenty-First Century*, by Thomas L. Friedman.** This intensive globalization romp vastly illuminates just how tiny the world's economic playing field has become. What has become unavoidably clear is that each individual's attempt at entrepreneurism immediately places one on an international footing. Along with that, the speed at which the convergence of technology and telecommunications allows one to run only gets faster and faster paced. The power and leverage that a cell phone, a laptop and an internet connection gives one cannot be fully communicated in my personal synopsis. All the more reason why this book is worth your time and energy to read and properly digest so that you will know exactly what macro and micro economic market forces one is up against. I don't believe one can gather enough relevant market data.

7. *The 10X Rule: The only difference between success and failure,* by **Grant Cardone.** This book has moved me more than most that I have read to date. Why? The man speaks his mind and comes from a posture of brutal and forceful practicality. Mr. Cardone radically shatters fanciful notions of the delusions the masses operate under. Failure, mediocrity, procrastination and so forth have been masquerading as success. He establishes as fact that the real reason most of us never achieve success is that we need to apply 10 times the passion, the commitment, the action, etc., to anything we currently desire. It is only upon applying un-relenting and never-ending energy to that which we intend to dominate that we ultimately ascend to the throne of success-ful conquest in your field of endeavor. The pace of economic change demands nothing less and external market change is not as important as working at implementing with speed your own personal goal and the expansion of your own personal economy. It is absolutely worth doing the exercises at the end of each chapter for proper digestion of his methods and ac-tion strategies for achievement. I notice that he has financial ideological differences with Dave Ramsey, businessman, author and radio host. I personally don't see a conflict be-tween the two so much as each is focused on a different fi-nancial aspect of the business equation. Ramsey is focused on the strict management of debt, an absolute necessity in a debt based economy. Whereas Cardone is focused on continual and never-ending expansion of the capacity to generate cash flow, also the lifeblood of any thriving business. Ramsey is about contracting bad debt and liability and Cardone is about expanding income and investment assets thru judicious use of

good debt. Both ideologies can and should achieve peaceful coexistence in the realm of personal and business fiscal discipline.

8. *Cashflow Quadrant: Rich Dad's Guide to Financial Freedom*, by Robert T. Kiyosaki with Sharon L. Lechter, C.P.A. This was the delicious sequel to the eminently successful Rich Dad Poor Dad. Mr. Kiyosaki conducts a superb illustrative dissertation on the internal structural rewiring everyone must perform to make the leap of faith. That being the leap from the employee and self-employed mindset of limits and scarcity across the Quadrant to a business owner and investor mindset with infinite potential and unlimited possibilities. He is very sober and sincere in outlining where the chips must fall. This is why I feel one really needs to read and reread all the books in the series to see the total entrepreneurial landscape for what it is and work thru all that it can be for you. It will only be scarier if we don't educate and prepare ourselves for a future of independence.

9. *Rich Dad's Before You Quit Your Job: 10 real Life Lessons every Entrepreneur Should Know About Building a Multimillion-Dollar Business*, by Robert T. Kiyosaki with Sharon L. Lechter, C.P.A. This book in his series is also worthy of note as he imparts more practical entrepreneurial lessons. As far as I am concerned one never can stop learning new lessons and in reality we trade up financial training wheels all the time. Please do not ignore his level - headed warnings as with any endeavor worth pursuing, it takes time to prepare oneself for great things. If it takes one

year, two years, five years to finally cut your employment puppet strings and become financially self-sufficient then so be it.

10. *Inc & Grow Rich: How To Cut Taxes 70% & Protect Your Assets,* **by C.W. "Al" Allen; Cheri S. Hill; Diane Kennedy, C.P.A.; Garrett Sutton, ESQ.** This book made with wide margins for making notations is a powerhouse of supremely practical information on living, breathing and sleeping inside an incorporated entity. Many case studies are given by this seasoned conglomeration of professionals astute in the areas of personal and corporate risk mitigation and risk prevention. They make it eminently clear that it is every citizen's right and duty to pay the least amount of taxes possible under IRS tax code. As well as simultaneously maximizing one's capacity to produce, protect and expand ones assets via legal leveraged corporate tax advantages. Forewarned is absolutely forearmed.

11. *The Power of Focus: How To Hit Your Business, Personal and Financial Targets with Absolute Certainty,* **by Jack Canfield, Mark Victor Hansen and Les Hewitt.** Of all the books that I would say to read and revisit out of this list, this book should be in the top 3 of most frequented. Why? It matters little if we proceed onto a path of massive influx of knowledge, strategize and formulate numerous tactics and goals, initiate massive action only to lose focus and momentum. Then our plane of opportunity taxes down the runway never to achieve lift off and crashes in the cemetery of lost hope and broken dreams. The biggest battles and the

war that must be won is not external, it is between our ears. The radical internal shifting required is identified, measured and streamlined into a consistently achievable process necessary to help us get from where we are to where we want to be. Not being able to finish this book will, in and of itself, speak volumes as to your ability to focus on anything long enough to make notable change.

12.   *Platform: Get noticed in a noisy world,* by **Michael Hyatt.** Mr. Hyatt's book is very simple and unassuming. However, don't think for one moment that his approach to this topic diminishes its powerful impact. What is immediately and clearly elucidated from the start to the finish is, you can establish a properly constructed medium for getting your message out and do so at a minimum of cost, time and energy. He does such an elegant job of demystifying social media and the way it should be dove tailed into any entrepreneur's plan for delivering value and exerting influence in the marketplace.

13.   *In Search of Quality: 4 Unique Perspectives, 43 different Voices,* by **Ken Shelton, Editor.** I greatly appreciate this book not just because of the interviews with business leaders from around the world but because it was done in dedication to Dr. W. Edward Deming. Dr. Deming is still considered the father of the Quality movement which, in part, inspired leaders of industry in post WW11 Japan to ultimately set the world standard for manufacturing quality for decades to come. What resonates with the leaders in this book and with me is that the Total Quality Management

(TQM) statistical improvement methodology can simply applied. Though complex in its application, the process simply asks; what is that rare 5% of improvements that optimizes whole business if everyone in the business works on it? This is a sweet spot that harkens to the Pareto principle that states that roughly 80% of the effects come from 20% of the causes. TQM drills down deeper to that 5% of one's business operations, that if qualitatively and quantitatively measured and incrementally improved upon, could reduce overhead costs, improve the quality of the goods and services produced and increase cash flow by 95%! This in my estimation is an exquisitely valuable and sustainable use of business time, energy and resources in leveraged proficiency.

14. *A Brief and History of Time*, by **Stephen Hawking.** Yes, I know this is well off the beaten path so allow me to explain its relevancy here. What I love about Mr. Hawking is his ability to take mind numbingly complex astrophysical and mathematical concepts and make them comprehensible and relatable to the layman or laywoman. In professional and business life, our capacity to take technical concepts and methods and make them uncomplicated for the people and markets we serve can, in and of itself, become a unique selling proposition. I use a book on more easily conceptualizing space-time as way to think thru how we can position ourselves to monetize any product or service that would improve the experience of the paying customer. Would they line up for something that would make things universally easier? Faster? Better? Less time consuming?

15.   *How I Became a Nurse Entrepreneur: Tales From 50 Nurses in Business,* **by The National Nurses in Business Association.** This book was what stoked the embers of entrepreneurism in me once again after experiencing burnout 15 years into nursing. Now that I am entering my 22nd year nursing, my world view has radically changed. At one time, I thought these 50 courageous nurses were also absolutely crazy. Now, I view them as more sane than most who are still crippled by fear and scarcity. I was at one time like the majority, bitter, frustrated, living and working only to fulfill someone else's dreams. Now, I am fully awake and courageously living my dreams because others before me dared to awaken and light a path that empowers.

16.   *The Coming Jobs War: What every leader must know about the future of Job creation,* **by Jim Clifton, Chairman of Gallup.** I have to say that this concise and well documented statistical work is worthy of any leader's consideration. If punch your own clock and are at the helm of your own financial ship then you are a leader. Leading yourself well comes before leading others and as a leader there is much to consider. With regard to the impact that your ability to attract and retain real talent, it becomes mission critical that leaders assess key present and future economic indicators. Mr. Clifton is the only author that I have ever encountered qualify Job Creation as a leadership skill, as a task that must be honed to mastery. In the not too distant future Job Creation, the ability to create more and more meaningful and challenging work, will become one of the top issues facing earths burgeoning human population. A radical concept and a worthy read.

17. *Business @ The Speed of Thought: Using a Digital Nervous System*, **by Bill Gates.** Who better to grant us a glimpse into our technological business future than the Software Architect himself! Since the book was published in 1999, much of what he postulated has already become a reality and we can say the only way many things will be. New terms and new corporate functions have had to be created as a result of so many converging technological platforms. Chief Technology Officer, Chief Information Officer, Social media Manager, Website Developers engaged in Search Engine Optimization and more on the way. The only thing that can be said consistently about digitalization is the how fast these systems and the core competencies surrounding their use becomes obsolete. The speed at which change is occurring means no one can afford to take their eye of the birdie. One cannot know enough about technology and what it can do, for and against your business interests. "Knowing your numbers" is fundamental to business. One must proficiently use technology to gather data every step of the way and understanding what it means so that it can be utilized to improve every aspect of your operations. This is what ultimately gives you a significant competitive advantage.

18. *Reading Financial Reports for Dummies,* **by Lita Epstein, MBA.**I find myself having to really focus and exert myself to fully benefit what the author is advocating. If I had to compare this book to anything, it is like a grueling series of boot camp sessions designed to cause radical transformation in bodies of thought. The end game of such exertions pays dividends in the form of flexing new monetary muscles.

Sweat equity in terms of heightened capacity for daily evaluations of your business weaknesses and the overall economic climate that your business operates in. I can speak from personal experience when I say, better to work harder here now to get and stay in financial shape than sweating bullets later in bankruptcy court from sloth and ignorance.

19. *The Organized Executive: New Ways to Manage Time, Paper and People,* by **Stephanie Winston.** I am so grateful that this book has been updated and I plan to buy the updated version to reflect changing technological trends. It is absolutely impossible to achieve anything meaningful if self-management is not approached in a methodical, coherent manner. Maximizing ones efficiency and effectiveness must now become an ongoing lifelong process. Long before one can expect to draw out greatness in others, it is essential to produce great things in one self. At the very least, greater productivity, creativity, utilization of time, essential protocols, strategies and processes that multiply time, energy, resources and people capital. Enough cannot be said about this subject area.

20. *Goals: How to Set Them How to Reach Them,* by **Zig Ziglar, A Nightingale Conant Audio Program.** I will admit right up front that I am a Nightingale Conant course addict!! I don't believe that one can work too much or too hard on developing the inner real estate of personal and professional development. Mr. Ziglar truly delivers on the title outlined and does it with southern charm! I find his message so uplifting that I still pull this course out every few months

and listen to it on audiocassette. Yes, though I'm dating my-self, don't get distracted by how old the content is because it is a true classic. Instead, engage your mind specifically on its enriching and delightful content. He simply helps one to practically see greater possibilities for themselves that is truly within everyone's grasp. Still some of the best motivational content on goal setting and goal achievement that is meant to be built upon.

21.   *Lead the Field,* **by Earl Nightingale, A Nightingale Conant Audio Program.** Mr. Nightingale not only has a compelling voice, but just as compelling a message of imparting success principles that can give lift to any who wish to take flight. (If you must know, yes I still have this one on audiocassette and proud of it!) This work delivers on its promise that if you listen to it just once you will be energized to achieve greatness! I love this as who of us is not meant for great things?

22.   *The Power of Visualization,* **by Lee Pulos, Ph.D., A Nightingale Conant Audio Program.** Dr. Pulos ad-vances some very exciting findings in this program that helps one to better harness the incredible powers of the mind eye. If anyone is incapable of engineering past mental roadblocks that are very much part of our past experience, then we can and will remain emotionally and fiscally handicapped despite marinating in amassing opportunities. Fortunately, it does not have to stay that way if we are committed to visualizing un-ending abundance and achievement for ourselves.

23. *Transforming Debt into Wealth: A Proven System for REAL Financial Independence,* **by John Cummuta, A Nightingale Conant Audio Program.** Mr. Cummuta is respectful yet firm in his conviction that it is impossible to create a life of real financial and spiritual wealth if one is bogged down by debt! His no nonsense, common sense methods for systematically living your life with debt was one of the hardest things I ever had to discipline myself to do. Seeing the world thru debt free eyes is difficult to describe!!

All that I can say is that you must hone your own powers of financial self discipline and massive action so as to experience this state for yourself.

24. *The Wealth Machine: How to Start, Build and Market a Debt-Free Business That Fits Your Life,* **by John Cummuta, A Nightingale Conant Audio Program.** I must give credit where credit is due! Mr. Cummuta loves to finish what he starts in sobering repose. He destroys a common myth that is still rampant in start your own business land, that of needing to acquire massive debt to build business credit just to have the satisfaction of running a high stress, high overhead business. Nay, nay! A debt-free business is the grand missing piece of the personal debt-freedom lifestyle that is so delightfully simple and non-puzzling. This concept should resonate with everyone living in a debt based society that still desires to build a self-perpetuating machinery of wealth.

25. *Your Money or Your Life: 9 Steps to Transforming your Relationship with Money and Achieving Financial Independence,* by **Vicki Robin and Joe Dominguez.** For as many ideas and approaches that I have pondered and explored, I must say that one is just not going to encounter another book quite like this one. The holistic approach these two authors take of translating the very concept of money into life energy and life values as basis for more effective decision making is a breath of fresh air. It provides an excellent set of guiding principles upon which to pause and reflect. This is most appropriate especially at time when everything in our modern society seems to be moving faster but not necessarily making us better off for it.

In Summary

I know, I know what some are saying already, that there are many, many other books just as good on the subject of finances, transformation and independence. True, all that this list of my favorite books is intended to accomplish is to start a life long journey of adventure and self-discovery. Along the way, it is my deepest desire that each individual will find that happy place. A place of positively changed circumstances, nourishing relationships and ever-expanding prosperity that will allow you to be, have and do more than ever before imagined. Continue filling the library of your mind with only the best and richest raw materials. Surround yourself only with those who desire for you to attain your fullest potential. Last but not least, give much thought and action to leaving the world a better place than you found it.